*Advance Praise for*

# more than a patient

"Jodi Taub transforms the chronic illness journey from isolation into connection. This compassionate guide shows that meaningful relationships and purposeful living remain within reach, even when living with fragile health. *More than a Patient* is the roadmap I wish I'd had when navigating my daughter's diagnosis. Jodi Taub offers hard-won wisdom that transforms chronic illness from a solitary struggle into an opportunity for deeper connection and purpose. This compassionate, practical guide turns survival into meaningful living—essential reading for patients and caregivers alike."

—**TRACY SHAW**, PhD, caregiver

"Jodi Taub eloquently shares her lived, personal experience as both a therapist and a patient battling an invisible, life-threatening immunodeficiency. She addresses one of the most important, yet complicated and ignored, aspects of chronic illness: relationships. Her book fills a large gap in the literature, and reading this feels like a friend sitting beside you. I will read it again and again. I am sure many will join me as well."

—**JENNIFER PATE**, MD, Psychiatrist
and patient with chronic illness

"*More than a Patient* is the rare book that bridges the professional and the profoundly personal. Jodi Taub writes not just as a clinician but as someone who has lived the complexity, grief, and grace of chronic illness. Having worked alongside Jodi in the chronic illness community, I can say that few people embody both compassion and conviction like she does. This book reminds us that while our bodies may falter, our capacity for connection—and for joy—remains infinite."

—**EVA MINKOFF**, MS, PCC, and patient

"As a therapist and a mom of a chronically ill young adult, I wholeheartedly recommend *More than a Patient*. Jodi's lived experience, wisdom, and care shine through every chapter. She also relays vital information on how to live your best life and thrive in your most important relationships. This book is a true gift for patients and the people who love them. I can't wait to share it with my community of caregivers and therapist colleagues."

—**JENNIFER KOGAN**, MSW, LICSW, RSW, and caregiver

"Jodi provides a relatable, approachable, and optimistic look at navigating life and love with a chronic illness. Her positive approach to tackling life's obstacles has been an inspiration and translates into each chapter. I highly recommend this book to anyone who has ever been or cared for 'a patient.'"

—**MARY YOUCH**, FNP-BC

"Jodi Taub offers a lifeline to anyone living with chronic illness, reminding us that while health may be unpredictable, we can always choose to strengthen the relationships that define our quality of life. With compassion and practical wisdom, this guide transforms isolation into connection and survival into truly living. An essential read for anyone navigating chronic illness."

—**MARIA N. ALIKAKOS**, DO, Psychiatrist

# more than a patient

*Building Relationships and Creating a Meaningful Life When You Have a Chronic Illness*

Jodi Taub, LCSW

WREN HOUSE
press



MORE THAN A PATIENT
Building Relationships and Creating a
Meaningful Life When You Have a Chronic Illness
*First Edition*

ISBN 978-1-967115-26-6 *Hardcover*
978-1-967115-25-9 *Paperback*
978-1-967115-24-2 *Ebook*

LCCN 2025927247

*For all who live with chronic illness*
*and those who walk beside us*

*When we are no longer able to change a situation,*
*we are challenged to change ourselves.*

—VIKTOR E. FRANKL

# contents

# foreword

*by Megan A. Ryan*

While I'd never wish my diagnosis on another person, I'm thankful for the healthy relationships I've developed with other patients who also have a primary immune deficiency. These are now lifelong friends, and we are on a journey together.

Being diagnosed with a rare or chronic disease does not come with an app you can download to help you navigate life. At times, we are awash in uncertainty about our health. It takes personal responsibility to become educated about your disease. But sharing knowledge about your diagnosis with family, friends, and other key people who are a part of your life can be hard.

You must determine how much to share and with whom to share. In opening up, you might find some relationships with friends or family members grow stronger.

Others may respond in a way that's undermining, cold, distant, or even worse, they disengage.

Navigating a complex diagnosis also means building a team of doctors and health care providers to support your physical and mental health. That takes time. And you must figure out those relationships too. How does each of those professionals communicate? Are they warm and engaging in the first interaction, or does it take time to feel comfortable and open with them?

While relationships can just "happen," for a lot of us, managing relationships requires an additional investment of time and energy on top of what can be an overwhelming or uncertain diagnosis. And yet the important people in our lives are so worth the investment.

Supportive relationships and genuine connection are critical for living better days with chronic health conditions. They help us maintain hope during difficult times, and they are vital to our long-term physical and emotional health.

This brings me to Jodi Taub, the author of this book. Jodi and I met through our shared involvement with the Immune Deficiency Foundation. She's been a speaker at conferences and online webcasts, authored dozens of articles, and more. Now, to support others, she has woven her lived experiences as a person who has multiple rare and chronic health conditions with her expertise as a mental health professional. In *More than a Patient*, we get the benefit and the insight of both perspectives.

I'm confident that the words in the chapters ahead will give you new tools and strategies to guide you and to make life with chronic illness more livable. The relationships we build and cherish with friends and family make us more than patients. We all need to be reminded of that.

I don't think of myself as a patient first. I think of all the other parts of my life and roles I live—wife, daughter, friend, neighbor, mentor, colleague. And I happen to have this complicated, frustrating, unpredictable, patience-testing, difficult-to-explain, underdiagnosed primary immune deficiency.

I'm more than a patient when I volunteer in support of my community, serve on boards of multiple mission-driven organizations, and advocate for the patient community. I'm more when I celebrate hard-fought successes, look back and see how I've grown as a person, and show up in all the ways I do for the people who matter to me. I'm curious and a lifelong learner, and I learn through living as well as from others. This book is an opportunity to learn from someone whose perspective spans two worlds: that of a patient and that of a mental health care provider.

Jodi tackles tough relationship topics so many with chronic illness face. She gives patients and care team members actionable ways to manage critical relationships during a journey with chronic illness. I know you will find comfort in her words. Throughout the book, Jodi's tips will challenge your thinking and demonstrate how connection and nurturing relationships improve health outcomes.

After nearly twenty-five years living with a primary immunodeficiency and other related conditions, I've cataloged many ups and downs. At times, my body felt like it was on the verge of imploding. Yet I've achieved some incredible professional and personal milestones too.

Whether at a high point or low point, I was thankful for the supportive community around me. I did not form this supportive network overnight. It came from nurturing relationships and finding the right people to engage and positively impact me along my journey.

For quite a while, I navigated my diagnosis with my health care team and immediate family. Then becoming involved with my patient community via the Immune Deficiency Foundation, I was able to meet fellow patients and their caregivers. I found people who are like me. There were others who understood what it was like to need regular infusions and have had similar medical experiences.

Now, I won't promise the first person you meet in a virtual or live gathering of your patient or caregiver community is going to be your new best friend. But by seeking out connection and talking and listening to many different people—maybe those with similar careers, interests, or hobbies—you will create a peer community you can turn to for mutual support.

Over the years, I sought out people my age—working professionals who made their diagnosis part of their life. I sought out people who loved to travel even though they had to manage their treatment schedule. I sought out patients who had a growth mindset and looked to the future even while living with a chronic disease.

Many of those patients did not look like me, some did not live in my city or even state, and most had different career paths, but I found the right people I could reach out to in times of cheer and periods of struggle. And importantly, they could also turn to me during rough patches and moments of celebration.

We can talk about our interesting body systems candidly and without judgment. It's validating when people in your life understand what you are experiencing. They listen and don't deny what you are telling them is your personal experience. They get it. For me, those relationships have been critical to living with chronic disease. I feel the strength of the community I've created and the camaraderie of shared life experiences. I do not feel alone.

You will experience some of that supportive energy in the pages of this book. When you get to the last page, take the title of this book as a personal challenge to get out there and live your definition of a full, satisfying (maybe sometimes messy) life full of people who support you through all seasons. Remind the world—and yourself—that you're more than a patient, because you are.

*Megan A. Ryan has transitioned from a career in auditing and consulting to serving in a number of volunteer board governance roles for mission-driven organizations. She's a lover of plants and flowers and walking. She can be found each morning walking the park and bayou trails near her home in Houston, Texas, and recently walked the Camino de Santiago in Galicia, Spain.*

INTRODUCTION

# a letter to those living with illness and hoping for health

Dear Reader,

I wrote this book as one of you, so I want to start with a personal note rather than a formal introduction. In more than twenty-seven years as a clinical therapist—eighteen of them working with patients and caregivers—I have braided together two lives. Moment to moment, I am living both my professional life working with chronically ill patients and my own daily reality as a patient who has primary immunodeficiency (plus many associated health conditions). I'm engaged in a lifelong battle with infections that are no big deal to a person with a healthier immune system. I'm still here to tell the tale, twenty sinus surgeries later.

My perspective as both patient and therapist has taught me something I know with unwavering certainty: the quality of your relationships will shape your experience and quality of life. This is especially so for patients living with chronic illnesses—and that's why I want to help you build and strengthen your relationships. It's the primary focus of this book.

Where would we be without family and friends—the people we live with, rely on, or just look forward to having coffee with? Your list might include a cherished partner, child, siblings, friends you've known since childhood, a new pal you met last month, and the sunny neighbor you bump into every now and again. They all matter in the human experience, especially for those of us who are living with complex medical conditions.

Some of our relationships might need help right now or at a future point, due to the normal shifts and changes life sends our way. This book focuses on managing relationships as an aspect of maintaining good mental health. I give practical advice and answer real questions people have about how to cultivate, improve, and enjoy relationships with all the important people who make up our community.

Research has shown that the best outcomes for patients depend on the quality of their social connections and relationships. Being "sick" inherently requires us to depend on others. Living in a Western society, where independence is rewarded and encouraged, can make us feel less capable when we turn to others for help. At the same time, research has shown that loneliness is an epidemic. Simply put, we need one another.

We didn't choose to be sick, but we can choose what we do with it. No matter your physical limitations, you can always find ways to connect with others, deepen relationships, and experience meaning. I say this as I currently sit in isolation, running eight hours of IV medication a day for a recent serious infection. And yet, I don't feel alone. I've spent hours working on this book, engaging with peers in online support groups, and texting with loved ones. The connection is there—even when I'm physically by myself.

This truth is the heart of why this book exists. Resilience doesn't mean bouncing back to who you were before illness. It means finding strength within yourself to make life meaningful despite pain—and doing so through connection with others. Building and nurturing relationships is ongoing work, but it is always worth it. So, let's begin.

## A Bit About Me

When I was asked to write this book, I wasn't sure how much of my personal story I should include. As a therapist, I've learned to wear a professional hat—to share only when clinically relevant and maintain strong ethical boundaries.

For years, I kept my own health journey offline. Before the protections of the Affordable Care Act, sharing my diagnosis could have affected my insurance eligibility. And more important, my work with patients was never about me, even though my lived experience gave me empathy and vulnerability few textbooks could teach. In recent years, I have been more able to share my experience. I'm grateful social media has helped patients find one another, and created an outlet for education and awareness.

Like you, I live this. My experiences are not just theoretical. They are my reality viewed through the additional lens of my clinical expertise. I was once told that people with my condition, common variable immunodeficiency (CVID)—didn't typically live past age fifty. I recently turned fifty. I currently live with multiple health care conditions, as a result of my primary immunodeficiency impacting so many of my organ systems. I spend about ten to twenty hours of my week attending doctor's appointments, getting nursing care, and carrying out my daily medical interventions.

## Baby, I Was Born with It

I may not look sick, but I am and was from the start—though no one had a name for it at the time. My parents used to say, "You were always sick; something was wrong with your immune system." My earliest memories involve illness, hospitals, and homebound days. I had the flu, infections, and constant stomach issues. Hospital stays were frequent. Yet, I was curious, bright, and determined. I made up for missed schoolwork when I could. I was always seeing some new doctor: allergists, gastroenterologists, endocrinologists, dermatologists, hematologists, urologists, sinus surgeons, and others.

Despite it all, I danced, earned top grades, and stayed socially active. I didn't let illness define my identity, even though it shaped every corner of my life. I was often homeschooled due to illness—in high school, then again in college. I was constantly underweight and plagued by gastrointestinal issues, which we casually called "a bad stomach." In my twenties, that diagnosis evolved into ulcerative colitis, and then acid reflux joined the mix. Respiratory issues followed. Then came the year I turned thirty, and I never got better.

That was the start of permanent symptoms. My sinus infection lingered for years. I faced surgeries, long-term antibiotics, and frequent hospitalizations. And still, at the time, primary immunodeficiency (PI) was hard to diagnose. There were no Facebook groups. Googling "PI" back then told me I probably shouldn't be alive. But in 2006, I finally got a diagnosis and started immunoglobulin therapy. It was the start of my post-diagnosis journey.

## Why This Book Matters

We find deep connections at the intersection of chronic illness, rare disease, and mental health. That's where I have spent the latter half of my professional life, supporting the mental health of people living with chronic health conditions—and those who care for them. It's been my great privilege to work with children, teens, and adults through individual therapy, couples and family work, and support groups.

Along the way, I published research and authored lectures in my area of expertise. I've given more than sixty lectures, webinars, and podcasts on chronic illness and rare disease. I also consult with therapists, psychiatrists, and other professionals navigating the complex realities of medical trauma, health anxiety, and emotional care.

My personal and professional worlds are inseparably intertwined in these pages. Yes, I write this as a clinician—but also as a patient, a partner, a caregiver, a daughter, and a woman who has navigated the uncertainty and vulnerability of chronic illness for decades.

I've been the sick kid, the adult who lost a job due to illness, and the person worried about insurance lapses. I've been cared for, and now I care for others—my parents, my patients, my community. I know how heavy it all can feel. And yet, I also know how meaningful and deeply human this experience can be when we let others in.

Despite all my ailments, I truly live a full life. I work full time—sometimes too much. I'm surrounded by an incredible community of friends, loved ones, and a supportive partner who is my caregiver. I still travel, cycle, swim, and dance like no one is watching. Despite all the pain and discomfort, I've never lost my zest for life. That's not to say there aren't days when I'd give anything to crawl out of my body and never again see another doctor's office. But I keep going, and that's entirely because of the people in my life who make it all worthwhile. My hope is that this book helps you strengthen your personal relationships. Believe me—it's worth it.

So, I dedicate this book to you and the entire community of patients living with chronic health care conditions, and to the loved ones who walk beside us. If my pain and hard-won resilience enables me to give you comfort, validation, or guidance, then this journey has had purpose.

Living with illness and hoping for health,

Jodi

# connecting with the people who matter most

ONE

# words that sting

## *A Guide for Handling Unhelpful Comments*

BEFORE WE DIVE INTO THE RELATIONSHIPS you have with friends, family, and other key people, let's talk about words. Oh boy, do words get in the way when you live with a chronic illness in a world full of people who have ordinary, only occasional health struggles. Living with chronic illness means regularly navigating not only physical and emotional challenges, but also the unintended sting of unhelpful comments from well-meaning people.

These remarks are often rooted in ignorance rather than cruelty, but they can still leave a lasting impact. Just about every person living with a complex medical condition has a story or two in this category.

When hurtful comments come from a stranger, that's one thing. But many of us have heard unwelcome, unfair, ill-informed remarks from people we love. This chapter is a practical guide for identifying how these comments affect us and how we might respond in a way that protects our well-being while also fostering understanding. It's a great warm-up for the rest of the book.

## Recognize the Impact

Sometimes, your body feels the weight of a comment before your mind even registers it. A spike in heart rate, tension in the shoulders, or the heat of frustration rising—these are signs that we're experiencing a fight-or-flight response. Before reacting, it's important to notice these signals and create a pause.

***Tip:*** Step away if needed. Go to the restroom, breathe deeply, or splash water on your face. Even a short break can help bring your nervous system back to baseline.

## Assess the Context

Not every situation calls for a response. It's helpful to consider where you are and to whom you're speaking. Is it worth correcting a stranger at the airport? You might want to save your energy. Ask yourself, *Is this a one-time interaction or an ongoing relationship?*

The answer can help you decide whether the conversation is worth having. If the person is family or a friend, maybe you have previously covered this same ground and they just need a reminder. Or does it warrant a longer conversation? Ongoing commentary can cause you to feel resentment that puts you on the road to disconnection and rupture within the relationship.

## Pause and Find Your Neutral

Before deciding how to respond, STOP. That is, use the STOP skill in dialectical behavior therapy (DBT). It can help you take a pause and make conscious choices during moments of emotional reactivity.

- Stop
- Take a step back
- Observe what's happening inside and around you
- Proceed mindfully

Responding in the heat of emotion can escalate a situation. Shift into neutral and then proceed with intention.

## Educate with Compassion

Many people don't know how their words land. If you have emotional bandwidth, use the moment to gently educate.

You might say, "I know that wasn't your intention, but I wanted to share how that comment feels on my end and offer another way to say it in the future." This approach defuses defensiveness and invites the other person into a space of growth and compassion.

## Reframe and Respond

You can use a classic cognitive behavioral therapy technique known as cognitive restructuring or thought challenging. Here's an example from my life, and it's a common one that chronic illness patients hear.

Someone says, "You're the busiest person I know."

My initial (defensive) reaction might be, "Yes, because you don't know anyone else who lives with so many chronic conditions and works full time."

That response may feel justified, but it's better to pause and use the STOP skill. I don't want to deepen feelings of disconnection.

Consider a reframe to an empowered response: "Yes, unfortunately managing my health care and working full time doesn't leave me with much leisure time. I'd love to see you though. My weekdays are packed, but maybe we can find a time on the weekend when I'm more rested."

This shift allows you to stay true to your experience while maintaining connection. While the defensive reaction is completely valid, reframing allows us to protect our energy while still advocating for ourselves.

### Rephrase Common Comments

When communicating about chronic illness, certain everyday phrases may unintentionally diminish what you're experiencing. Take a look at the table below. People who use these phrases may not realize the hurt they can cause. The goal is not to shame anyone but to offer a roadmap for more compassionate communication. I hope the suggested alternatives validate your experience, and open space for understanding and support.

| | Why It's Harmful | Better Alternative |
|---|---|---|
| "But you don't look sick!" | Dismisses invisible illness and implies you're exaggerating your condition | "How are you feeling today?" or "Is there anything I can do to support you?" |

| | Why It's Harmful | Better Alternative |
|---|---|---|
| "At least it's not cancer." | Minimizes your experience by comparing it to another illness, which can invalidate your pain | "That sounds really hard—how are you coping?" |
| "You just need to think positively." | Oversimplifies your experience and subtly shifts responsibility from external circumstances to your mindset | "I'm here for you. What has been helping you get through this?" |
| "You're too young to be sick." | Implies that illness has a certain look or age limit, thereby questioning the legitimacy of your struggles | "I didn't realize how much you're dealing with. Thanks for sharing that with me." |
| "It could be worse." | Invalidates your pain by forcing a comparison, which can discourage further sharing and connection | "I can't imagine how tough this must be for you. Would you like to talk about it?" |
| "Have you tried...?" | Leads to unsolicited advice instead of offering support or a listening ear | "Would it be helpful if I shared something I read or tried, or do you prefer I just listen?" |

Do you feel validated by this list? We can take a moment to sigh because we hear these phrases all too often. But let's also take the opportunity to start productive conversations. Maybe someone in your life would appreciate seeing this page to better understand your point of view. Whenever you can, invite those around you to more thoughtfully engage in how they support you. Helping others learn to reframe can be a double win. It empowers you, and your community of friends and family, to communicate with empathy and understanding.

## You Don't Look Sick

"You don't look sick" is a commonly heard phrase—just four words but they sting, and they're worth exploring more deeply. It may be intended as a compliment or to cheer you up, but it puts you in the position of defending yourself. It's like saying, "I don't believe you." It denies your reality, and invalidates your circumstances and what you're really going through.

My patients say they're also hurt by others' suggestions to utilize certain diets, supplements, and or medical interventions. These are unlikely applicable to their specific health conditions, even more unlikely to miraculously cure their condition or change their outcomes. If this sounds familiar, know you're not alone. Even when suggestions are offered sincerely, it can still feel hurtful.

Whether someone doubts your illness or suggests a fix, the resulting feeling is the same. That person is misunderstanding and invalidating your experience. It can feel like the person is passing judgment, as if your reluctance to stick to a certain food fad or exercise regime makes you responsible for your symptoms.

Taken to an extreme, it's called traumatic invalidation—when a person's feelings, experience, or identity are repeatedly, intensely minimized or rejected. This damaging behavior causes anger and resentment. It can strain relationships and cause further disconnect. This can happen with our closest friends and family members.

So how should you respond and use the encounter as a teaching moment? It's best to have a preplanned statement. You could say, "I know I might not look sick, but actually, that's not how I feel. And the way I feel may not be visible to you." For myself, I could say that what you don't see are my chronic fatigue, pain, and discomfort, and the hours I spend on my medical care routine, including mandatory rest. Here's a scripted response that might help:

I know it may seem like you're complimenting me, but it serves as a reminder to those of us who live with chronic health conditions that some people or physicians may not believe us or think that we are exaggerating.

## Saying No to the Magic Cure

Many patients and caregivers living with chronic health care conditions experience uncomfortable confrontations that start with someone asking, "Have you tried..."

What usually follows is the suggestion that a certain food, diet, exercise routine, or wellness practice could miraculously cure your condition if only you would try it. The suggestion that someone else knows how to better manage their complex health condition is my patients' number one hurt—full stop.

We, the people living daily with chronic health conditions, do fervently wish for a cure. A survival instinct burns brightly in us all. Our friends and family also want us to find a cure. That's why they make these recommendations, however off-base.

It may be momentarily pleasant to imagine there's a magic, off-the-shelf solution. The honest truth, however, is that for many of us, our illness—at least right now—can only be managed. It can't be cured. In fact, there are thousands of rare conditions for which there are no treatments, let alone cures. Many of us live with hereditary and genetic diseases that will be present with us for the whole ride.

As for me, my immunodeficiency is not going anywhere, no matter what I do. Right now, there is no cure and that's a tough pill to swallow, no pun intended.

But even after you have accepted that reality, the suggestions may keep coming from people you know and from the global wellness industry, which is worth more than $5 trillion according to one estimate. Prior to getting diagnosed with an immunodeficiency, I went down that rabbit hole, looking for answers. I tried it all and actually felt worse until I was properly diagnosed and could begin treatment. I understand all of this now, but at the time, I did not. I was vulnerable and desperately seeking a cure. I know this may resonate with many of you reading this book.

While your upset is valid, make a good faith effort to educate loved ones and repair relationships. Try the techniques I share in this chapter. You might show this section to a loved one who has suggested magic cures. Explain how this creates a rift and ruptures trust. Why? Because it doesn't respect all the earned wisdom you have about your chronic condition.

Though they are only trying to help, ask them to hear you on this point: You are the expert in your own health. Tell them you rely upon your own judgment and the judgment of trusted medical specialists who understand your condition and know your medical history. The partnership between you and your medical team gives you the best chance at managing your health with success.

You can tell the friend or family member that it's OK if they don't always understand how you feel physically and emotionally. But ask them not to invalidate your experience. Let them know that acknowledgment and supportive statements really help. These are some examples I like to hear:

- "I really respect how much you get done despite your health condition."
- "I appreciate your positive attitude even though I know you go through a lot."

We may not be able to control the words of others, but we can learn how to respond and care for ourselves when faced with unhelpful comments. Whether you choose to walk away, speak up, or teach through compassion, you are reclaiming your power. Every small interaction is an opportunity to shift the narrative around chronic illness—one conversation at a time.

Not everyone will get it. Their worldview on chronic health conditions may be too rigid and resistant to change. A degree of acceptance may be needed on your part but also set your boundaries. You can choose not to discuss your health with certain people, especially if their behavior impacts your health.

Happily, others may have the capacity to make changes over time, if you can lead them down the right path. The next time a comment catches you off guard, pause, breathe, and remember that you deserve to be heard, seen, and respected.

TWO

# friends

Friendships brighten our days and fortify us in difficult times. From childhood to old age, friendships can be among our most rewarding relationships, and they are extremely important for patients living with chronic health care conditions. Humans are wired for social interactions.

Cherished friendships color our lives through shared experiences, common interests, and milestone events. But not all our friendships will go the distance. That's true in the best circumstances and can be especially so when one of the friends faces a chronic illness.

A life-altering diagnosis can shift your priorities and your sense of identity. You might not feel up to the usual social activities. Your health might cause you to cancel plans or go home early. In short, needs and expectations change, and sometimes friendships fade. If this has happened to you, you likely felt misunderstood or disappointed by your friend's lack of support.

Don't give up on them though. Friendships are so important and valuable that I encourage you to max out on friendships—old and new. Many distanced friendships can be saved with effort and flexibility on both sides.

Unfortunately, some friendships do end, often when our lives and needs change. Being someone's friend is a choice, and just like any other relationship, a friendship requires commitment, nurturing, and care. Fortunately, you can choose to be a friend again and again throughout a lifetime.

In this chapter we discuss friendships that end, maintaining and strengthening current bonds, and the impact of forming new alliances.

## Grieving a Lost Friendship

As a result of chronic illness, many of us will lose friendships. Some friends may not be able to tolerate a friendship with someone who is sick. They may have unresolved trauma from personal experiences with a loved one's illness, or perhaps fears about their own health.

Friends of convenience may be insensitive or unwilling to invest in a friendship that has changed because you no longer meet their needs. A friendship can be situational, based on a shared activity like tennis or working for the same employer. If you have to stop playing tennis or you leave that job, you won't see the person on a regular basis. Some people may not want to invest in the relationship if you no longer have the shared experience that first bonded you.

Such friends drift away because friendships take effort and prioritization. It's not unique to the chronic disease community. This also occurs when people graduate from college, move to another city, have children, get divorced, and so on. It can feel very personal, but not all friendships are meant to be long-term, and it's OK to let some friendships go.

It hurts to lose a particularly close friend or someone you have known a long time. You thought this person was your ride-or-die. They shared so many of your highs and lows. You never anticipated that the relationship would or could change.

But here's why they sometimes do: For a long time, your life experiences were relatable to each other. You might have struggled side by side with romantic breakups, career challenges, marriage, divorce, or loss of a loved one. Now, only one of you has a chronic health condition. It's a new wrinkle, and it can break the long-held bond.

Chronic illness can change our identities, our capabilities and, ultimately, how we live life. Depending on your condition, you might experience brain fog, fatigue, and pain—all of which make it hard for you to be as present as you once were. Enduring friends will take this truth on board. Some friends simply can't or won't cope with the shift.

They cannot accept how your life has changed and what that means for you. Why? Some just don't understand chronic disease and don't want to learn about it. Your friend might refuse to accept that your chronic disease can't be cured or easily fixed. Younger people especially might struggle with this because they associate illness only with grandparents and senior citizens. Meanwhile, you are working hard to adjust to the reality of managing a chronic condition and its roller coaster of unexpected flares.

No one is perfect, and you don't want to hold your friends to a strict set of requirements. Our friends' varied strengths, personalities, temperaments, and even quirks are what make them fun to be around and a source of security in tough times. But you might decide to end a friendship that's no longer supportive. If so, give yourself permission to grieve.

Although this can be painful, remind yourself that the glass is half full when it comes to friendships. Invest in friends who want to show up. Some old and steadfast friends will meet you where you are and accept all the realities of your illness. With some effort on your part, new alliances might form and widen your social circle. We can make friends at every age and stage. Look for opportunities to join local volunteer organizations, book clubs, school-related groups, places of worship, and social clubs.

## Maintaining Existing Friendships

The good news is that many existing friendships, even if you encounter conflicts or struggles, are well worth saving. Most people want to help and stay connected, even if you're facing health challenges. Think about the special people in your life, their strengths, and why these relationships are worth the effort. Make this an exercise in prioritizing your most valued friendships and how to strengthen these important connections so they have a place in your life. Here are positive steps to take:

- Tell your friend how much you appreciate them and look for ways to gain more social time. Put time with friends on your to-do list and value it as much as other important responsibilities, like caring for your physical health. More social connection time is an investment and creates a foundation for securing mental health and stability.

- Explain—or re-explain—your limitations to important friends. Ask willing folks to meet you on your terms. No one wants to be seen as rigid or a burden, but with a little more explanation and a direct request, the right people (those for whom you are a priority) are likely to react in a way that shows they care and value having you in their lives.

- Keep health updates simple and educate valued friends about what I call "inconsistent capabilities." In other words, unpredictable symptoms cause your abilities to fluctuate—something able-bodied individuals might not understand. (One day you are up for a long walk; the next day, you aren't.) Medical terms are familiar to you, but they won't be for everyone. Be patient and consistent in your messaging. Share the same information more than once and forgive them if they don't retain everything you said last time. Ask gentle questions to check their understanding of what you said. Dialogue can be clarifying for both of you.

- Let others know how you want to be supported. Don't assume they know how and what you need. Utilize your friends' strengths. Some friends excel at processing feelings, whereas others are ready to jump in to do the practical work. Ask honest questions. Let friends know you want them to support you in a way that feels comfortable and natural to them.

- For chronically ill people who are single, and for those in high school and college, friends may serve as a supportive network in place of family members or partners. Be conscious of overburdening one friend, to avoid burnout or resentment. Make an effort so the relationship feels reciprocal and about more than your receiving caregiving.

- Recognize when you need support from a mental health care professional. If you are experiencing clinical symptoms of anxiety, depression, or post-traumatic stress disorder (PTSD), it's OK to talk to your friends about how you are feeling. However, a mental health professional is best when you need help managing these symptoms.

- Enthusiastically support your friends and show up for them in the ways you can. It feels good to reciprocate and know your support is valued, too. Don't minimize what you bring to the table.

### Making New Friends

There's no denying that it's harder to form friendships when we're older. Experiencing "firsts" with friends—first day at a new school or first time on the swim team, for example—during key developmental time periods can create deep bonds. But we can stay in the friendship game throughout our lives. We humans are biologically wired to want social connection—from super-close friends we've known for years to casual pals we sit on the sidelines with at a child's soccer game.

You might feel a bit awkward setting out to make some new friends. Try approaching it from a different angle by focusing on the interests and activities that give you purpose, meaning, and satisfaction. Chronic illness can upend your sense of purpose if you can't work in the same way, or you don't have the free time or physical abilities necessary to pursue the hobbies you once enjoyed. This can lead to isolation, loneliness, and shifts in identity.

We all need to have a sense of purpose outside of managing our health care. Find something that deeply interests you and get creative about how you can do it, even if it has to be with some modifications. Take an online class, join a book club, or reengage with a childhood hobby. Reassess what you enjoy and find a way. Through those absorbing experiences you are likely to meet people who are similarly passionate about your favorite thing to do—a great way to spark a new friendship.

Studies have shown that everyday interactions with a neighbor, a fellow dog owner, or a store cashier can be quite beneficial to your state of mind. You get to engage with others, but without the complications or judgments that tend to go along with more intimate relationships. Less personal information is shared, and in that moment, you don't have to claim the identity of a chronic disease patient if you don't want to. You can just be a person at the dog park or the customer in the checkout line who likes dark chocolate. Take advantage of these little connections—you might find they boost your mood and brighten your day.

### Finding New Friends Who Are Also Patients

If you're managing a chronic illness, one benefit of forming a new friendship is that your new friend will meet you—and see you—as you are now with your current limitations and (don't forget) hard-won resilience. People who live with the same or similar medical condition can become especially deep and lasting friends.

Personally, I think these peer-to-peer relationships are vital. Having a friend or community of friends who just get it can be very powerful. I find I can be vulnerable and not worry about the other person judging me or my abilities. It's a wonderful, very welcome kind of freedom. How can you get started?

- Start with a trusted patient advocacy group, and look for events, private social media groups, online forums, and other support groups. You could have the opportunity to meet in person at a conference on rare diseases or to connect with someone on the other side of the world without ever leaving your couch. Knowing that these special friends are just an instant message away can make all the difference when feeling isolated at home or in a medical facility.

- Volunteering for a disease-related nonprofit organization can link you up with new people and deepen your connection to the patient community. Take the opportunity to utilize your strengths and showcase your talents, especially if your condition has limited your ability to work or be active. As a bonus, your involvement with an advocacy group can help you manage your health care. These groups offer educational opportunities and resources for better disease management. They also provide avenues for advocacy so legislators, health care providers, and researchers hear patient voices when making decisions.

## Navigating Bumps in the Road

Whether friends are old or new, it's normal for friendships to hit a rough patch. If your friendship needs repair, remember that everyone makes mistakes in relationships. Try not to let resentments fester. If you feel upset with your friend and it is impacting the relationship, give them the opportunity to mend the conflict. Consider how your chronic illness may be impacting your friendship and be open to resolving the situation. (Is it something they said? Refer to the previous chapter about how to handle unwelcome comments.)

Have you been feeling left out? Living with chronic health care conditions makes cancellations inevitable. Remember those "inconsistent capabilities"? Friends might make assumptions about what you can and can't do. Eventually, some friends may assume you will decline their invitations and just stop asking. This can be so hurtful, though your well friend has no ill intent.

Do you prefer to be invited so you have a choice? Be proactive by telling your friends to please extend the invitations and not to be dissuaded if you can't always make it. Or maybe you prefer to get together during times when you feel up for it. In that case, tell your friends you'll reach out to them and that you'll understand if they can't always make it on short notice.

If you miss an event, explore alternatives with your friends. Could you join virtually if you're feeling unwell? Can you reschedule that girls' night out or tennis match? Put it on the calendar!

## Animal Friends—the Benefits of Pets

No chapter on friends would be complete without mentioning our beloved pets. I write this with my dearly beloved Mr. Beatle in mind—my loving dog companion of nearly fifteen years. He was with me through many moments when I didn't feel well, always by my side. He was my trusty companion and nurse. I will always be profoundly grateful for his time on Earth.

If you have had a pet, you know the powerful impact they can have. Pets often become family, providing unconditional love and bringing joy, structure, and meaning to everyday routines. Many can relate to the simple pleasures of seeing their goofy expressions or celebrating when they follow commands or manage a successful bathroom trip. These small moments can spark joy and connection.

### *Physiological and Emotional Benefits*

Research has shown that interacting with pets has measurable physiological benefits. Petting an animal has been found to reduce cortisol levels, thereby decreasing stress. Conversely, it increases oxytocin—the same "bonding" hormone that connects mothers to infants. Additionally, spending time with pets can elevate levels of serotonin and dopamine, both of which are neurotransmitters associated with mood regulation and feelings of pleasure.

More recent studies show that pet ownership is particularly beneficial for individuals managing chronic illnesses. A 2024 study found that pet companionship provides psychological benefits comparable to close human relationships and significantly enhances life satisfaction—especially for those facing long-term health challenges. These findings reinforce what many of us with chronic illness already know intuitively: that our pets are not just animals but essential sources of emotional stability.

### *Pets as Mindfulness Catalysts*

Caring for and interacting with pets can also mirror the effects of mindfulness. Mindfulness is the practice of focusing one's awareness on the present moment with compassion. Pets ground us and help draw us into the here and now, whether through playful engagement or the quiet act of sitting together. Studies have shown that pet ownership fosters emotional regulation.

### *Social and Relational Benefits*

Pets enhance social connection. If you've ever walked a dog in your neighborhood or gone to a dog park, you know animals are natural conversation starters for people. Shared affection for animals can create immediate bonds between strangers and foster casual interactions, which boost mood and combat loneliness.

In some cases, these interactions evolve into deeper relationships. Friendships may develop among pet owners who frequent the same parks or clinics. And of course, pets themselves—with their quirks and personalities—can inspire laughter, storytelling, and connection. Many of you may have already discovered that special connection among pet owners.

### *A Sense of Purpose and Pain Management*

Pets offer a strong sense of purpose, especially for individuals who live alone. Caring for a pet introduces a sense of meaning beyond one's health challenges. On difficult days, knowing your dog or cat needs to be fed or walked gives you something important to show up for. Many of us have our own caregivers and might feel that at times we burden others. Being responsible for a pet demonstrates we can be dependable caregivers, too.

Research supports this experiential truth. In a qualitative study exploring the role of pets in chronic pain self-management among older adults, researchers found that pets facilitated emotional coping, behavioral activation, and routine regulation. Participants described how their pets offered comfort, encouraged gentle physical activity, and served as therapeutic distraction from pain. Pets helped reduce isolation and gave structure to the day, which aligned with cognitive-behavioral pain management strategies.

Even brief moments of activity—like getting up to feed or play with a pet—can provide a sense of accomplishment and resilience. Micro routines can help break the cycle of inactivity and despair that chronic pain and illness sometimes bring.

Pets also encourage time outdoors, which has well-documented benefits for mental health. As the National Institutes of Health has noted, small interactions with animals and nature help reduce stress and improve mood.

### *Addressing the What-Ifs of Pet Ownership*

Some may worry, *If I can barely take care of myself, how can I care for a pet?* That's a fair concern—but many find the emotional benefits outweigh the risks. Support systems can be established with dog walkers, neighbors, or friends who are happy to help with short-term care of your pet, especially during health flares or medical procedures.

For those with allergies, it's important to consider nonallergic pet options. Also, maintaining good hygiene for pets going outside is also important. Wiping your dog's feet when coming in from outside, and appropriate bathing, can help keep you and your pets healthy and safe. With preparation and community support, pet care becomes manageable—and the rewards are measured in joy, comfort, and connection.

THREE

# dating

I DON'T HAVE TO TELL YOU THAT DATING CAN be tricky even when both parties are healthy. On a first date, you might wonder, *Do we have anything in common?* When one party has a chronic illness, it adds a whole other layer of complexity. The usual dance of boundaries grows increasingly complicated. Dating is a weeding-out process, and it's not always just about chemistry and connection. Both parties face potential rejection. But the person living with a chronic condition encounters inner turmoil. *Will my health problem be a deal-breaker? Should I keep it a secret for a while?*

Sadly, a chronic condition *will* be a deal-breaker for some people. I won't pretend otherwise. It's painful to be rejected for any reason, but to be rejected because of a disability we have no control over carries its own kind of hurt. But here's another truth: there will be people who accept you, admire your strength, and won't see your illness as a deterrent. The challenging part is navigating the messy middle—figuring out whom to tell, when to tell, and how to tell.

You may have already chosen how open to be about your condition. Some live loud and proud, embracing their disease community in a public social media feed. Others are more private, choosing discretion and waiting before they share with anyone, including potential partners. There is no "right" way to do this. The right way is whatever works for you.

### Surviving the Apps

Dating culture has changed dramatically in the last few decades. With one click someone can decide if you're right or wrong for them. Ghosting has become an unfortunate norm, and those living with chronic illness might feel particularly vulnerable—especially if someone disappears after you've revealed your health condition.

For many years, I've worked with patients navigating these challenges—and I've been there myself. I didn't meet my long-term partner, Sean, until I was forty-two.

I dated and experienced rejection, and yes, we met on a dating app—our modern cliché.

I know the pain of being rejected because of my health. Some people were reluctant to date me due to concerns about long-term outcomes. These experiences still sting. But for every rejection, there were gains. As a bit of encouragement, I can tell you I am now surrounded by peers and patients who are happily partnered. Many of those partners serve also as their caregivers, and not one has ever considered leaving because of their partner's health condition. We all deserve companionship. Having a chronic illness may be challenging, but it doesn't mean you can't find love.

Chronically ill or able-bodied, we all face health problems at some point. Choosing the right partner can make this journey more fulfilling and less lonely. Having someone to lean on—who will step in when needed—can improve your quality of life.

Navigating new relationships when you're managing symptoms, energy limitations, or unpredictable health changes requires vulnerability, intentional communication, and thoughtful self-awareness. If you have already jumped into the dating pool, you know that real-life challenges and meaningful possibilities arise when chronic illness intersects with romantic connection.

## The Vulnerability of Disclosure

One of the most emotionally fraught questions is this: *When do I tell someone I'm dating about my illness?* There's no universal answer. For some, it may feel necessary to share early on to filter for potential partners who are genuinely supportive. For others, it may feel safer to wait until trust is established. Either approach is valid. What matters most is that the timing aligns with your comfort level and emotional safety.

Disclosure can bring up fear—of rejection, of pity, or of being misunderstood. Yet for many, it can also be an opportunity for intimacy and authenticity. When you share your health story in a grounded way, it can be an invitation for your partner to share more of themselves, too.

How do you prepare for these important conversations? It's worth doing a deep dive for yourself so you're not caught off guard and can approach the moment with clarity and confidence. Anticipate questions your potential partner may ask. A predetermined script is helpful, and you might consider preparing a few for various circumstances. Start by explaining what your condition is, how it impacts you, and how you modify your life to adapt. These are usually the issues most people want to know. Here are some scripted remarks to get you started on what you might say:

> "I have [*insert condition here*]. Although there's no cure, I follow a treatment plan to keep my symptoms in check. That involves [*insert details here*]. I still tire easily, so I try not to overschedule myself. I prioritize rest. For the most part, it's under control. I keep up with my doctor's appointments so I can lead a full life with some modifications."

> "I have [*insert condition here*], which limits my ability to [*insert detail here*]. I work hard to stay as physically able as possible, and I try not to strain myself with daily activities. I get tired easily, so I avoid [*insert detail here*]. I have made modifications to my work life and personal life to make things easier. For example, [*add more info here*].

People may ask questions like these: "Can you have kids?" "Do you want kids?" "Will you be able to work?" "Will it get worse?" Anticipate these questions, even the most sensitive ones, and prepare compassionate, firm responses that reflect your boundaries.

For example, if someone asks if you can have kids,

you might use humor: "Well, I'll ask my future spouse!" Humor can lighten the discussion and redirect the conversation away from questions you need not answer in the early stages of dating.

We've talked a lot about the extra burdens, but there's a silver lining. Disclosing your chronic illness can be a great way to filter for emotionally mature, secure attachments. Someone who has a rigid, predetermined list of wants in a mate might quickly rule you out. That's OK because such a reaction reveals someone who is unable to handle complexity, tolerate uncertainty, or look past your health condition.

Someone who is relationship-oriented and looking for a real connection will give you a chance in spite of your health condition and will admire your strength in facing adversity. They will recognize that the traits you've developed—resilience, emotional regulation, and perspective—make you a strong partner. The right person will stay. They'll learn, listen, and adapt alongside you. Most important, they'll see your worth without needing you to hide or shrink the truth of your experience.

And if it's a true match, this person also might be willing to accept a role as caregiver, if needed. I share more on that in Chapter 5 about partners and spouses as caregivers.

## *A Three-Point Plan for Dating*

1. **Decide when to tell.** What are your boundaries about sharing your health condition? You might decide to share only after seeing someone regularly. If you have only a few dates, it might not be worth getting into. Others prefer to share early to rule out potential obstacles. Know where you stand.

   If your condition is visible, you may have fewer options to delay disclosure. Still, you get to decide how much you share and when. It's OK to start with broad strokes and fill in details later.

2. **Decide how to tell.** Choose a calm, open setting—not at the end of a date or in passing. You might ease into it when a lifestyle difference arises such as food restrictions or schedule needs. Some people lead with humor or frame it as part of their life story.

3. **Decide which narrative to tell.** It's important to share your story on your terms in a way that makes sense to you. Be prepared for judgment. Able-bodied individuals may say things that are unintentionally hurtful. This is to be expected—it often comes from ignorance, not malice.

   Emphasize your strengths and adaptations. For example, you could say something such as, "I like to be active, so when I feel up to it, I go for bike rides and attend Pilates classes." Share that, with some modifications, you can still lead a full life.

## Identity, Body Image, and Desire

Chronic illness can change the way we see ourselves—and how we imagine others might see us. Fatigue, weight changes, medical devices, scars, or limitations may affect confidence and body image. Some may worry, *Am I still attractive? Desirable? A whole partner?* These fears are deeply human.

You are not less lovable because of your condition. In fact, the depth, resilience, and insight you bring to a relationship may impress and delight your able-bodied partner. Anyone who's dating takes a risk in the hope of finding companionship and love, maybe even for the long-term. The brave act of dating also serves to affirm your worth and worthiness. Yes, you deserve all the goodness that can be had in a healthy, happy partnership—even if you're also dealing with a health condition.

Desire doesn't disappear because of illness; nor does the need for connection, flirtation, and sexual expression. What may change is the pace, the context, or the form. Communication, creativity, and a sense of humor can go a long way in cultivating a romantic and sexual life that honors your body's realities while nurturing emotional intimacy.

## Navigating Practicalities

Chronic illness often adds practical considerations to dating. These can include the following:

- Planning around flare-ups, fatigue, and the need for rest
- Managing medications, diet, or mobility needs
- Navigating medical care, related paperwork, costs, and caregiver schedules

It may take some time to develop the skill of being clear and direct about your needs—without overexplaining or apologizing. It's OK to say, "I'd love to see you this weekend, but I need a low-key evening," or "My energy isn't great tonight. Can we talk instead of going out and reschedule for another night that works for you?" These boundaries won't deter the right partner, who will appreciate your clarity.

## The Role of Support and Community

If you still feel a little shaky, try talking to other patients who have experience in the dating world or healthy relationships. Try support groups, social media communities, or friends who "get it." You may find helpful scripts, shared humor, and inspiration. You are not alone in navigating this.

The foundation of strong partnerships lies in mutual respect, honest communication, and shared expectations. These principles hold true whether you're five months into dating or fifteen years into marriage.

### Redefining What Dating Success Looks Like

Dating with chronic illness may look different than the mainstream narrative—but that doesn't mean it's less meaningful. Success isn't defined by frequency of dates, adherence to social norms, or having a perfect body. It's about finding connection, feeling seen, and building a relationship in which both partners can grow.

- **Build your self-worth outside of dating.** Confidence doesn't come from others liking you—it's about knowing your own value.

- **Know your non-negotiables.** You deserve respect, support, and curiosity—not pity or avoidance.

- **Don't minimize your experience.** If someone makes you feel like "too much," that's information about them, not you.

- **Date with discernment.** Pay attention to how someone responds to your health needs. Do they ask questions and make space for accommodations, or do they disappear when things get real?

- **Clarify your needs.** What accommodations do you need for dating to feel safe and enjoyable?

- **Stay grounded in your values.** You're not auditioning for love—you're cocreating it.

Dating is a filtering process—and you're filtering, too. Look for someone who shows up, listens, and doesn't treat your condition as a problem to fix. Remember that the traits of someone who would accept your chronic health care condition—loyalty, flexibility, kindness, a giving spirit—also make for a good partner. Look for someone whose presence feels like a relief, not a risk. Secure partnerships are consistent and feel safe. Love is not reserved for the healthy. And your story, exactly as it is, is worthy of being heard—and cherished.

Everyone's dating journey is different. You may or may not be ready to date, and that's OK. Maybe it's not a good time because you're facing a difficult health flare-up or are newly diagnosed. If now isn't the time, put this chapter on pause and revisit it when you're ready.

FOUR

# long-term relationships

Dating progresses to something more profound when you decide to make a commitment to another person, be that in marriage or a long-term partnership. Having a loyal, loving romantic relationship is one of life's joys. A spouse or partner fills many roles through the years or even decades. Your shared history together can be a source of fun and connection, and it can also steady you with strength and support in difficult times. Not surprisingly, research shows supportive relationships are associated with better psychological and medical outcomes in people managing chronic illnesses.

Ideally, while you and your partner were dating, you discussed and worked through some of the issues surrounding your chronic condition and how it affects daily life. You might already know that facing a health struggle together can deepen your bond with a partner, but it also can overwhelm someone who was not expecting to serve a caregiving role. Where is your partner on this sliding scale? When you're ill, are they a supportive presence from the sidelines (and you prefer it that way), or have they already stepped in to directly care for you? We talk in depth about caregiving partners and spouses in the next chapter.

Did your diagnosis come before you formed the relationship, or was it thrust upon you both at the same time? A surprise diagnosis can be shocking to both parties and leave the healthier person wondering what the future holds and whether they can accept the knowns and unknowns that lie ahead.

Breakups are common and half of all marriages end in divorce, so it's no surprise that it takes work to sustain relationships. Many want to take steps to maintain relationships but just don't know how. If you're enjoying the promise of a long-term relationship—or in an existing relationship that needs some tending—here are five areas to work on together:

1. **Take steps to prevent caregiver burnout.** Your partner may at times become your caregiver. (I

prefer "care partner.") Assess what kind of care or assistance you need and how much your partner is willing and able to provide. What are your partner's strengths? No one can be everything and do everything.

Reach out to friends and family members, too, and ask for their support. Having several care partners can reduce strain on your relationship. It decreases isolation and keeps you connected to a wider community of people who care about you.

2. **Maintain a partnership that's about more than caregiving.** Prioritize your partnership—and your partner—even though managing chronic illness can sometimes be a full-time job. Schedule date nights and look for other ways to connect. Your partner will have their own stressors in life. Ask what kind of support they would like to receive from you.

   Show interest in their lives. Spend leisure time together. Keep an open dialogue about how to maintain your sexual connection. If your physical condition is limiting, find new ways to connect. Remember that able-bodied partners must do regular relationship maintenance, too.

3. **Acknowledge your partner's experience around your illness.** When you are struggling with a serious health condition, you have physical symptoms and often feel emotional turmoil. Your partner, as a caregiver and observer, has their own emotional experience. They may feel guilty about the good fortune of their stable health. Because you're suffering physically, they might feel they can't ask anything of you. This can lead to feelings of anger, resentment, and even loneliness.

   Remember that care partners might feel helpless and a loss of control when they witness your physical struggles. They might not get the validation and understanding they need from others. Try to be empathetic. Encourage your partner to connect with supportive friends, and to do activities that refresh and recharge.

4. **Establish a good communication style to use when your illness flares.** All of us have moments when our symptoms are better or under control. When you are experiencing a flare-up, it is easy to indulge in a negative thought spiral. Be aware of how this may impact your partner and learn how to communicate what you need in these stressful times.

5. **Be proactive about cancelled plans and other inevitable situations.** It's the night of an event you have both been looking forward to, but you're not feeling well. Is it OK for your partner to attend without you? When do you need space or need some extra help? Communication is key and can decrease unnecessary conflicts, especially if you talk through some of these scenarios before they happen.

   Research shows that patients who have supportive care partners have improved physical and mental health outcomes, and feel more satisfied with their lives. Fortunately, the benefits of these long-lasting, committed partnerships can flow in both directions. Many care partners find in their relationships a sense of purpose and meaning, which can increase their happiness and yours.

## How Are You "Attached"?

You have probably heard of attachment theory and attachment styles. Attachment theory was developed in the 1980s by pioneering psychiatrist John Bowlby, and psychologist Mary Ainsworth later expanded on the theory. Attachment theory explains how early caregiver relationships shape patterns of trust, intimacy, and emotional regulation across the lifespan. Attachment styles—secure, anxious, avoidant, and disorganized—describe consistent ways individuals seek closeness, respond to stress, and navigate relationships, including romantic partnerships and caregiving bonds.

This can be a helpful lens for examining how you connect with a long-term partner and how that person connects to you. Books have been written on attachment theory and romantic relationships. *Attached: The New Science of Adult Attachment and How It Can Help You Find—and Keep—Love* by Amir Levine and Rachel Heller helped popularize these concepts for a wider audience, applying theory beyond the parent–child bond to explain how attachment styles influence intimacy, trust, and communication in adult partnerships.

### Attachment Theory and Styles

Psychologists have identified four primary attachment styles:

- **Secure attachment**: Characterized by comfort with intimacy and autonomy, a secure style develops when early caregivers are responsive and consistent. Adults with secure attachment generally trust others, regulate emotions effectively, and build stable relationships.

- **Anxious attachment**: Marked by heightened sensitivity to rejection and a strong desire for closeness, this style emerges from inconsistent caregiving. Adults may become preoccupied with relationships, worry about abandonment, and need frequent reassurance.

- **Avoidant attachment**: Rooted in caregiving that is emotionally unavailable or dismissive, avoidant attachment applies to individuals who often downplay emotional needs, value independence, and may struggle with vulnerability or intimacy.

- **Disorganized attachment**: Associated with frightening, chaotic, or neglectful caregiving, this style reflects a mix of anxious and avoidant behaviors. Adults may experience difficulty regulating emotions, and feel conflicted about closeness and trust.

These attachment patterns do not determine a person's future but provide insight into how individuals may respond to stress, illness, and caregiving relationships. Understanding one's attachment style can help patients and caregivers navigate the challenges of chronic health conditions with greater awareness, flexibility, and resilience.

The takeaway I offer is that the traits of a securely attached partner are valuable in general, and particularly so to someone who has medical vulnerabilities. A securely attached partner feels comfortable with intimacy, can regulate emotions effectively, and tends to be more consistent and responsive. Feeling connected to your partner improves brain integration and can heal stress and trauma.

A secure partner...

- Offers reassurance instead of judgment.
- Listens with empathy and doesn't rush to fix.
- Can tolerate the discomfort of unpredictability.
- Has capacity for flexibility and caregiving, if needed.

Difficult times can test a relationship to a breaking point, but they also can be an opportunity to see strength and resilience in action. The most stable couples "turn toward" each other in moments of vulnerability, according to professionals at The Gottman Institute, which is known for its research-based approach to couples therapy. "Turning toward" means showing interest, validating feelings, and offering consistent emotional support. Does your partner turn toward you when you're honest about your health? Do they disappear, deflect, or judge?

Wherever you are in your relationship journey, know there is a way to build a relationship that lasts. The proof is found in the real lives of many patients who have built long-lasting, in-it-for-the-long-haul partnerships.

# getting real about caregiving relationships

FIVE

# when your partner or spouse is your caregiver

WHILE CAREGIVING FOR A CHILD COMES naturally, caregiving for a partner or spouse requires adjustment, as it is not an assumed part of a romantic relationship. When we're falling in love with someone, most of us don't envision a future that includes driving them to doctor's appointments, directly caring for them when they're ill, or sitting bedside when they're hospitalized—at least not until old age. But, at some point, your partner may become your caregiver. That reality can be daunting but also deeply bonding when grounded in love and reciprocity.

Maybe you both started out equally healthy, or perhaps you began your relationship already knowing one of you lives with a serious health condition. Even if your partner was aware of your illness, that was just a snapshot in time. Health is a moving target. Chronic health conditions can be inconsistent, and one's level of functioning can change. You and your partner may face the reality that you need caregiving sooner rather than later.

One's health limitations reverberate and affect critical aspects of day-to-day life, such as these:

- Money and finances if the patient must stop working or needs to work less
- Distribution of household tasks like cooking, laundry, and cutting the lawn
- Parenting and responsibility for hands-on childcare
- The ill person's ability (or inability) to care for aging parents
- Companionship when one partner has less energy, is ill, or can't travel or attend important events

Any of these can be difficult to work through, and it's common that couples must deal with several or all of them at once. Here's where it pays off to have selected a securely attached partner and together established a secure relationship in which both people feel emotionally safe. No question, these situations are still complex and difficult for both parties. But in a secure relationship, partners have more tools for dealing with a health flare-up, a surgery, or a worsening condition.

In a less secure relationship, the patient managing an illness might feel abandoned if their partner maintains a social life they can't share. Of course it's always a balance, but the healthier partner should feel comfortable being social and taking part in events, even if their partner can't always attend. Putting unreasonable limits on the healthier partner can contribute to caregiver burnout.

A mental health care professional can help couples work through the varied impacts on their household and relationship, especially if one partner must temporarily or regularly serve as a caregiver. Couples can learn to understand and accept the role of the "thirds"—activities your partner does solo and people they see without you. Could a partner's continued social life hurt the relationship and lead to breaking up? In my experience, illness does add strain, but it is rarely the only reason a relationship does not succeed.

## What If a Woman Can't Be a Full-Time Caregiver?

Though progress has been made, our society still often looks to women to assume the caregiving role for their partners and their children (and later, their parents). By nature, and often by nurture, women typically shoulder more than their share of the domestic burden, especially when it comes to caregiving responsibilities. From pregnancy through birth and breastfeeding, women fill biologically assumed roles. And they also work outside the home in huge numbers.

But "having it all" and doing it all isn't realistic for most women—even those who are healthy and full of energy. Arlie Hochschild writes about this in her 1989 groundbreaking work *The Second Shift: Working Parents and the Revolution*, which explores the burdens women took on as they came into the workforce and were still expected to maintain their domestic responsibilities. Hochschild describes how women, compared to their significant others, put in a month more of work per year while carrying most of the emotional weight of domestic life.

I know those unrealistic cultural expectations fall hard on women who are also managing rare and chronic illnesses. We may not be able to meet everyone's expectations at home and at work. Rather than be full-time caregivers, we may need others to take care of us sometimes—and that person may be a partner or spouse. This can substantially impact a woman's self-esteem and identity. It can upset our sense of balance in the relationship and how things ought to be. We all want to be able to care for the ones we love, including our partner. But because of the unpredictable nature of managing a chronic illness, we may not be able to show up in all the ways that healthier women can for children, parents, and partners.

If this is you, it's important to accept the reality that your limits are your limits. Your partner can care for you some of the time without the risk of losing the essence of your romantic relationship. You can still show up for those you love in meaningful ways, even if it's at a lower volume and doesn't fully meet societal expectations, which—reminder—are difficult for all women. Your gifts and strengths persist despite your chronic illnesses. Whatever restrictions have been forced on you, know that you are still a valuable partner, mother, daughter, and friend.

## Yes, Men Can Be Caregivers Too

Many of the men I have worked with in my practice and support groups claim that caregiving did not come naturally but took some time to get used to. It's the little things, like being less comfortable than women in asking for time off from work because of caregiving responsibilities. Men don't typically talk about caregiving with their friends. This reluctance to share with others can leave them feeling isolated and lonely, which can lead to anger, resentment, and disconnection from the relationship. Some may experience clinical manifestations of anxiety, depression, and PTSD.

I strongly encourage male caregivers to find a support group or an informal social media group. Simple acknowledgment of similar peer experiences can decrease isolation, provide insight, and validate and normalize their experience. As for those who step up to the challenge, I've encountered many men in my practice and support groups who have found a sense of purpose in caregiving.

Taking care of a partner in this way can enhance connection. This additional dimension can bring you closer to your partner if you learn how to incorporate it in a way that feels right and balanced to both of you. Perhaps it must be experienced to be fully understood, but knowing your loved one can really count on you is the essence of romantic attachment and partnership.

## What about Sex?

Illness impacts sex lives in many ways. Patients may be medically restricted, feel less interested, or be physically unable, depending on the health flare-up and symptoms they're experiencing. The healthier partner may feel rejection and then stop initiating. The unintended consequence is that the lack of interest then makes the chronically ill partner feel unattractive and undesirable due to their medical condition.

This unpleasant cycle forms, leaving both partners disconnected from intimacy, and sex just does not happen. This does not need to be the case. Talk about how to make time for intimacy. Discuss the best time of day or day of the week for you. People managing a medical condition are often tired or don't feel well. Be honest about symptoms so your partner knows it's your gastrointestinal woes, not your lack of interest, that are causing you to say, "Not tonight."

Spend time on the building blocks of closeness and connection—gestures like holding hands, making eye contact, and offering compliments. This is really where the basis of sex begins. If you go through a dry patch, talk about it. Remind your partner that you are still interested and that you will let them know when you feel more up to it. Take stock of how you spend your time together—medical appointments don't count as dates. Make sure you are spending quality time together, as best you can. Your caregiving relationship and your romantic relationship are separate entities, so attend to them separately.

There are some additional issues to address and work through together. Be on the lookout for established patterns that are no longer working.

## Division of Household Labor

When one partner needs to pause and drop out of household responsibilities, chaos might ensue. Dishes pile up, the garbage can overflows, and the car doesn't go for an oil change. No one likes it when the household isn't running as usual. So as not to overburden the healthier partner, determine and then prioritize the "musts" for you and your partner. Focus on strengths and what each of you reasonably can do.

Strategize your distribution of chores in two zones: one for when you're in good health, and another when you're experiencing a flare-up of symptoms. Be practical and solution oriented. Could one of you manage health care paperwork and the other partner do appointment scheduling? If you're supposed to make dinner but are feeling unwell, you'll order takeout instead. Can you ask a neighbor to pick up your child after sports practice? Don't wait for a crisis before creating a plan. Being prepared helps you keep important items from falling through the cracks. Revisit the plan occasionally to make sure it's still working for both partners and current conditions.

## Expand Your Support System

It makes sense that your partner would be the main character in your support system. As convenient and comfortable as that may be, it's time to widen your network. Reaching out to other friends and family gives your partner a break and opens the door to other people who have unique strengths.

You might have a friend who's a great cook (and is willing to drop off dinner once in a while) or a family member who's a whiz at sorting through medical paperwork. Another pal with free time could take you to an appointment if you aren't up to driving or going alone.

You'll likely find that your friends and family want to help and will respond if you ask them for specific kinds of assistance. Getting outside support reminds you that you're not in this alone. That wider circle also can guard against caregiver burnout, which can cause your partner to feel disconnected from you and to experience mental health symptoms, isolation, and loneliness.

## Watch Out for Guilt and Shame

Our rational minds know we shouldn't blame ourselves for having a serious health condition, losing independence, and needing help sometimes. But we still might feel guilty about what we can't do. And our partners might feel ashamed of their resentment when we're "missing out" on an important event. We're in the soup together on this one.

Imagine the whole family is attending a birthday party and you're not. How can you be honest about what you want while giving your partner full permission to enjoy the party and not feel guilty or angry you're not there? It gets complicated if you say, "yes, go," but secretly hope they will stay home with you. That's confusing for your partner. Honesty can help break the guilt-shame cycle. Build trust with your partner and eliminate confusion wherever you can. If the two of you disagree about how to handle an event, look for alternatives and make your non-negotiables known.

Through it all, aim to remain a giver and hold your partner in high esteem. Be their biggest fan. Find ways to contribute even though you have health flare-ups. Small efforts and minor shifts matter. Valuing and appreciating each other are potent fuel for keeping a relationship going.

SIX

# when your caregiver is your parent

IT'S SAID THAT IF YOU SUCCEED AT PARENTING, you will eventually put yourself out of a job. Parents set out to raise a child to become independent and self-sufficient, though the road may be longer, with more twists and turns, if that child or young adult is coping with a serious medical condition. Independence remains the goal, but it's trickier for everyone involved.

As the facilitator of caregiver support groups for many years, I have had an up-close view of the challenges parents go through, especially those who assume the primary role as caregiver to a chronically ill child. No parent wants to watch their child suffer, and all parents want their children to lead healthy prosperous lives.

Medical caregiving provided by parents calls for a delicate balance. On top of their full-time job being Mom or Dad, they must remain vigilant to ensure the child gets the necessary medicine, tests, medical care, and more. Often, they serve in the role of a nurse who enforces daily medical routines the child resists. If the child must take special precautions, like avoiding crowds or contact sports, the parent has the job of enforcing unpopular restrictions. They also manage the associated administrative tasks, such as scheduling appointments and picking up prescriptions. The weight of these demanding responsibilities can result in burnout.

If you're a young adult receiving care from a parent, know that this relationship makes important contributions to how you view and manage your health condition. Is your caregiving parent detail-oriented and often checking that you're following your care plan? Or maybe your caregiving parent has pulled back over the years, giving you increasing independence. You might be eager to shift the balance and take more control of your health care management. Or it could be your parent is pushing you to take the reins but you're unsure about being fully responsible for your medical care.

Of course, a young child who has chronic illness will require medical caregiving from a parent. But as the child grows up, the level of caregiving provided can evolve in a variety of ways, depending on the severity of the condition and its symptoms. The handoff from parent to child can take time and test both parties.

### Balancing Parenting and Adolescent Independence

As children with chronic illnesses transition into adolescence, fostering independence becomes crucial. Research emphasizes the importance of preparing adolescents for self-management of their health. Strategies include the following:

- **Collaborative planning:** Parents should involve teens in health-care decisions. The parent should clarify their role as parent versus medical advocate.

- **Risk assessment:** Together, parents and teens can talk with physicians about what level of autonomy is safe and age-appropriate. Teens should understand boundaries without feeling there will be a consequence to their health by participating in "normal teen" activities.

- **Reinforce trust**: Parents should reinforce that they believe in their child's capabilities and are there when needed.

- **Revisit roles**: Parental involvement can adjust as flare-ups, life changes, or developmental transitions arise.

- **Shared nonmedical experiences**: Parents and teens should make the time they spend together about more than managing the chronic condition. Everyday fun—movie nights, outings, or shared hobbies—can rebuild joyful connections.

### How Long Should Parents Be Caregivers?

Transitioning to adulthood can be stressful and exciting all at the same time. Parents and their young adult children need mutual grace and understanding as they navigate these waters. It's not as simple as just turning eighteen. Parents may stay involved in the management of the chronic condition for a number of years before the person is comfortable handling things independently. Early on, a young adult may reach out to friends for support. Later, the source of hands-on, reliable support may come from a committed partner or spouse.

Over time, young people take strides toward more independence and rely less on their parents. Young adult patients need to learn how to do the following:

- Set up appointments and meet with their physicians on their own
- Turn to friends and significant others for medical support when parents can't step in
- Make wise lifestyle choices, which may impact their health

I recommend young adults and their parents discuss this important transition. Ease the process by establishing some guidelines together. One question is, *When should this shift occur?* For some people, high school or college graduation can be a natural time to take on more responsibility, especially if the patient is planning to leave home. But even if a patient still lives in the family home—as some do for financial, emotional, or medical support—he or she will want to play an adult role in their care.

## Community Is Key

Young adult patients don't need to go it alone, even as they're trying to become independent of Mom and Dad. Adopt these two best practices: (1) Establish a community of people who can help when you need it. (2) Know when to ask for help. Spending quality time with your support system decreases isolation and supports improved mental health. Aside from your parents, who in your life might be willing to pitch in? Who is reliable and how would you like them to help? Let friends know how you would like to be supported. This helps set some expectations and gets you the assistance you really need.

While you once relied solely on one or both parents, now you might build out a deeper bench of people—each with their individual strengths. Some might be able to help with practical tasks, such as picking up a prescription, making a meal, or driving you home after an appointment or procedure. Others may be great company when you need a distraction, while you're managing chronic fatigue, or during times you're not feeling well enough to go out.

## Taking on Case Management

For most young adults, their parents also served as their medical case managers who handled or assisted with scheduling appointments, insurance reimbursement, and making health care decisions with your physicians. Taking over all these tasks and responsibilities can feel overwhelming at first.

The good news is your parents are probably experts at this point and can serve as helpful guides. Start a dialogue in a nonjudgmental manner about how to take on some of these responsibilities.

One of the best recommendations for anyone with a complex medical condition is to create and maintain an updated document that captures all your medications, health care conditions, surgeries, and physician's contact information. This will save time at doctor's appointments—especially when seeing a new physician—and can be shared with others when you need someone to advocate on your behalf.

## Inviting Significant Others In

Are you dating someone seriously, or taking the next step to live together or marry? A long-term romantic relationship can also prompt a shift in who takes the lead in supporting and caring for you. Naturally, some caregiving responsibilities may fall on your partner. Take things slowly so your partner is not overwhelmed. Start a dialogue about how comfortable they may be regarding certain aspects of your care. Keep in mind that you and your parents had many years to adjust to your health care regime.

As you begin to include your partner, let your parents know you have a new source of support. This can be a relief to your parents, who may have trouble letting go and fear you are taking on too much responsibility for yourself. After perhaps a couple decades of caring for you, this could be a big change for them. But if you talk about the transition together and go at a comfortable pace, these steps will well equip you for taking good care of yourself.

As children with chronic illness grow into young adulthood, caregiving roles often shift but rarely disappear entirely. Parents may still support their adult children by coordinating medical care, managing medical records and other paperwork, providing transportation to appointments, and lending a hand with the tasks of independent living. This ongoing involvement can blur the lines between medical caregiving and parenting.

Caregiving at this stage is often invisible and misunderstood. Support groups for long-term or lifespan caregivers can be a powerful source of validation. Many parents experience grief over unmet expectations—for themselves and their children. There's often a sense of conflict between wanting to protect their child and wanting them to live a full, independent life.

Therapy may also help caregivers process their evolving identity and the emotional toll of continuing to provide intensive support when peers are moving on from active parenting roles. Your parent's role can evolve from hands-on care to a supportive, advisory position. They can step back with intention—and you can step up—while maintaining a trusting relationship. Thank them for their years of care and for adapting to your growing capacity.

## Putting Yourself in Their Shoes

Parents who are caring for a chronically ill child often experience burnout. A study involving 206 parents of children with chronic illnesses found high levels of caregiver burden and associated depressive symptoms. Common symptoms include these:

- Increased fatigue
- Decreased motivation
- Withdrawal from relationships and other personal commitments
- Decreased feelings of joy and fulfillment
- Lower frustration tolerance and increased irritability
- Clinical mental health symptoms, including anxiety, depression, PTSD, and medical trauma

Caregivers may experience profound loneliness—not only from physical isolation but also from the emotional perception of being alone in their responsibilities. Studies during the COVID-19 pandemic revealed that loneliness in caregivers can mimic the brain's response to physical pain and is associated with increased anxiety and depressive symptoms.

## Aging Parental Caregivers

Many chronically ill adults are still cared for by their aging parents. This is especially true for single individuals, who might rely heavily on their parents for support and medical advocacy. These relationships can be deep and foundational.

When the roles reverse—when you begin to care for the people who once cared for you—it can feel disorienting and deeply emotional. If the transition is sudden due to illness or loss of functioning, the adjustment can be especially overwhelming. Give yourself time to grieve and process the emotional weight of this change.

It takes time to adjust to the loss of a primary caregiver. When that loss is sudden—due to death, illness, or other unforeseen circumstance—the emotional impact can be particularly profound. You're not just grieving the person's absence, but also the support, routine, and security they provided. This compounded loss can feel incredibly destabilizing. Tapping into your extended support network is essential for ongoing care.

While no one can truly replace a primary caregiver, building a small network of support can help ease the transition. Identify a few friends or family members who each bring different strengths—someone who can help with post-surgery pickups, a person you trust for health decision input, and somebody who can simply be there when you need emotional support.

Maybe your mother was always by your side during medical procedures. Now, that role might shift to a partner, sibling, or close friend. It's not about replacing this important person in your life—it's about adapting and leaning on a team instead of one individual. Your support system will look different than it did and maybe even different than what you expected—and that's OK.

Sometimes the people we assume will step up won't be able to, and others may surprise us with their generosity. Be open to receiving support from unexpected sources: neighbors, members of a faith community, colleagues, or even online groups. It takes courage to ask for help. Building this kind of safety net can make a world of difference in your well-being, allowing you to move forward with more confidence and stability.

## *If You're a Caregiving Parent of an Adult Child*

Unlike parenting younger children, caregiving adult children involves more negotiation, boundary setting, and communication around autonomy. It's crucial to revisit the caregiving dynamic as the child matures:

- **Reevaluate roles and responsibilities.** As adult children become more capable, consider shifting from doing to supporting. Ask what they want help with and respect their preferences.

- **Encourage autonomy with support.** Young adults coping with chronic illness may struggle to balance independence with fluctuating capacity. Caregivers can support responsibilities without taking over.

- **Plan for the future.** Consider long-term care planning, including guardianship, disability accommodations, and access to supportive services.

- **Acknowledge caregiver grief.** Grieving the loss of a typical parent-child relationship as the child transitions into adulthood is valid. So is the ongoing fear for your child's well-being.

SEVEN

# being a caregiver when you're chronically ill

MANAGING YOUR OWN HEALTH CONDITION while caring for children, a spouse, or aging parents creates a unique and often overwhelming set of circumstances. How can you take care of someone else's needs when it's already difficult to care for your own?

The answer lies in having a plan, setting realistic expectations, and putting that plan into action. Without a plan, everything can quickly spiral when, say, a child gets sick, your spouse has a health emergency, or your aging parents need urgent care.

Research shows that individuals who manage chronic illness while also taking on caregiving roles experience heightened stress, burnout, and emotional strain as compared to caregivers without chronic conditions. First and foremost, it's essential to accept the reality of your situation. You may not be able to take on some of the roles society expects. If you're immunocompromised, you won't be the one caring for a child with the flu or COVID-19. If you have physical limitations, you likely can't assist your husband with heavy lifting if he's sprained an ankle.

Others may expect more than you can give. As discussed throughout this book, some able-bodied individuals may never fully "get it." They see you functioning day to day and have no idea how much effort it takes just to manage your own life. If your spouse or child is suddenly ill, you might experience a double whammy of feelings. First, there's guilt because you aren't able to help in all the ways you would like to. And then you may be judged by others for not doing more, especially if you're a woman. Women disproportionately carry caregiving responsibilities, and often report greater emotional and physical strain, highlighting a gendered aspect of caregiver burden.

Despite societal expectations, acknowledge that if you can't care for yourself, you can't care for others.

Seek the backup assistance you need and find ways to be supportive without putting your own health at risk. Not surprisingly, caregivers report reduced quality of life and increased fatigue when expectations outpace their capacity, especially in the absence of adequate planning or support. Choose to pitch in for tasks that align with your strengths and feel manageable.

These are some strategies for coping:

- Set realistic expectations for yourself and communicate. Be clear, and don't overcommit.
- Create a care plan for your loved one.
- Remember that your experience as a patient gives you something akin to an informal doctorate in medical case management. That's a valuable skill set you can apply here, especially in case management.

## The Sandwich Generation

Many people experience caring for aging parents while raising children at the same time. It's a challenge for anyone, but it can be especially daunting when you're already managing your own chronic health condition. Family members might lean on you for medical decisions, documentation, and crisis management—roles that can quickly become overwhelming. For a chronically ill patient, being part of the "sandwich generation" means facing unique emotional, logistical, and financial pressures.

If you're stuck in the sandwich generation, here are some tips for managing:

1. **Divide tasks fairly.** If you're handling medical coordination, be clear about how much time it takes. Setting up doctor's appointments, follow-ups, and dealing with paperwork can be a full-time job. Make sure others pitch in, to avoid resentment.

2. **Have a backup plan.** Let your family know your health must come before caregiving responsibilities. Create a contingency plan for when a flare-up prevents you from fulfilling your caregiving duties. Studies underscore the importance of proactive planning and task delegation to reduce caregiver overload and ensure continuity of care.

3. **It's OK to say no.** Sometimes, you simply can't take on the role of caregiver. This might cause

conflict, so work with your family to find realistic, sustainable solutions.

4. **Don't put yourself at risk.** It's natural to want to help aging parents but not at the expense of your own health. Use affirmations such as these:

   "My parents wouldn't want me to jeopardize my health to care for them."

   "They've always prioritized my well-being. I'm honoring them by protecting my health."

   "Though I can't be physically present at the hospital or other high-risk environments, I can support them in other meaningful ways."

   Write down these affirmations so you can use them as reminders and during a sympathetic nervous system fight-or-flight response, which can cause a flurry of negative thoughts and anxiety. Just reading such statements can provide a parasympathetic nervous system reaction, which can be grounding and calming. Using therapeutic coping skills can be helpful in the face of crisis. Refer to some of the techniques outlined in Chapter 10.

5. **Anticipate family dynamics.** As parents age, old sibling roles and rivalries may resurface. Conflict is common. Address issues calmly with empathy and hold your boundaries. Be prepared for certain family members, especially those who have downplayed your condition, to impose unrealistic expectations. Therapy, both for the individual and for the family, can help process these emotions. You can also seek advice from an attorney, financial advisor, or clinical case manager for the elderly. A lot of good resources are available for caregivers of aging parents.

6. **Watch for emotional triggers.** For a chronically ill patient, caregiving can bring up past medical trauma. Here's an example: Kendra, a patient living with multiple health conditions and complex medical needs, visited her father, who was hospitalized in the same ICU where she had once been critically ill. PTSD symptoms resurfaced.

   With support, she used her set of reliable coping strategies and individual therapy sessions to manage her symptoms and process the experience. I also encouraged her to bring up this experience in her support group. The validation from her peers allowed her to acknowledge that she no longer felt alone.

Experiences like Kendra's are common. Caregivers who are responsible for patients facing life-threatening health events, in particular, show a high risk for chronic PTSD symptoms, especially when personal medical trauma is involved.

Similarly, parents may experience trauma related to their child's medical experiences. Pediatric medical traumatic stress (PMTS) can lead to symptoms akin to PTSD. Witnessing a child's pain, enduring emergency interventions, or being dismissed by providers are all traumatizing. Someone experiencing PTSD symptoms requires professional mental health support services, so seek assistance if you have an experience like Kendra's.

### How to Avoid Burnout

If you are both patient and caregiver, burnout can creep in quickly. Caregiving often disrupts routines, especially during emergencies, so maintain nonnegotiable self-care practices like medical appointments, daily hygiene, and essential treatments. Take breaks. You may need an occasional day off from thinking about or carrying on routines for your loved ones. This is not only acceptable but will also sustain you, maintaining your energy for the long haul.

Caregivers may grapple with these emotions:

- **Shame**—feeling inadequate in managing caregiving responsibilities
- **Guilt**—believing they could have prevented health declines
- **Anger and resentment**—toward the illness, system, or even the loved one
- **Loneliness**—feeling isolated due to caregiving demands
- **Emotional exhaustion**—chronic fatigue from continuous caregiving

These emotional responses are common and valid. Recognizing them is the first step toward seeking support and implementing coping strategies. To mitigate burnout and emotional distress, approach your role with intention and compassion. Seeking assistance from family and friends can be a vital next step. Establishing emergency plans with relatives or trusted individuals offers peace of mind.

### Being a Caregiver for a Child Who Has a Medical Condition

Care responsibilities are often unbalanced in families, so sharing tasks with a partner or co-parent deters resentment and strengthens the caregiving structure. Try to play to each of your strengths. Maybe one of you excels at medical paperwork and the other is great at handling medical appointments. Delegating practical duties—such as grocery shopping, carpools, or billing—through delivery services and shared apps can free up valuable time and energy.

Setting limits is essential. You'll get more burned out if you overcompensate and don't set boundaries. Children thrive within structure, and modeling healthy boundaries teaches them resilience.

Maintaining connections through caregiver support groups, especially those accessible online, offers validation and insight. There is relief in talking to someone who simply "gets it." Caregivers in many support groups I lead describe how powerful it is to have found a group of people who understand without needing long explanations or fearing judgment. They say they hadn't realized how much support they needed until they received it—and that having space to reflect helps them understand they had been operating in survival mode for far too long.

Self-care doesn't require grand gestures. Even taking a short walk, listening to music, or texting a friend can provide emotional release. These practices demonstrate to your children that prioritizing mental health is not only acceptable, but also essential. Similarly, relationships with partners, other children, and close friends need attention. Though time is limited, honest communication about your availability can sustain meaningful connection.

It's also crucial to acknowledge your emotional landscape. Feelings of guilt, frustration, or resentment do not make you a bad parent—they make you human. Suppressing these emotions can lead to shame spirals. Instead, bring them into the open with trusted confidants or professionals.

Family and friends may not always understand the kind of support you need. Initiating conversations about your preferences—emotional, logistical, or practical—can lead to deeper understanding and more helpful assistance.

Draw on your individual strengths and let those guide your caregiving identity. You may not feel strong every day, but there is value in the perseverance you demonstrate. Caregivers can let go of the impossible standard of doing everything—and doing it perfectly. Reframe what "enough" looks like. It can preserve your energy and your relationships.

### Mental Health Support for Caregivers

Accessing mental health services, such as individual, family, couples, and group therapy, can provide coping mechanisms and emotional support. How can a therapist help? Therapists help identify the difference between everyday stress and clinical mental health symptoms. Family therapy can assist in navigating sibling dynamics, co-parenting, or lifestyle adjustments, such as one parent pausing work. Couples therapy may strengthen communication and help resolve resentment.

Some caregivers hesitate to seek help due to stigma or guilt. They worry it seems like complaining when a loved one is ill. But therapy is not about blaming—it's about strengthening your ability to cope and thrive.

I have been leading caregivers support groups for partners and parents for many years, and I consistently witness and receive feedback about how beneficial it is. The caregiver role is such a unique experience that most of us did not anticipate. Loneliness and disconnection come from others who do not validate or understand. Establishing a peer connection is vital. Plenty of caregiving groups, especially virtual, are out there.

Mental health care also improves your capacity to problem-solve, supports flexibility during difficult transitions, and reinforces social connectedness. According to a 2020 study on rare disease and caregiver satisfaction, emotional support and companionship are strongly linked to better mental health outcomes.

All of us, at some point, will have a loved one who needs our help. You can make a meaningful contribution toward the person's care, but you cannot and should not do it all. Look for alternatives, modifications, and creative solutions. Part of the job is explaining that to other people and maintaining your boundaries.

# managing health and building resilience

EIGHT

# working with doctors and health care providers

LIVING WITH A CHRONIC ILLNESS REQUIRES ongoing interaction with health care providers, insurance companies, hospital systems, and specialists. These relationships can be supportive and lifesaving. They also can be emotionally fraught, especially when communication breaks down or when patients feel dismissed or misunderstood. Establishing and maintaining effective, collaborative medical relationships is essential—not only for receiving proper treatment but also for preserving your emotional well-being.

If you are a patient in the United States, you likely know the frustrations embedded in our complicated medical system. Wherever you live, you may have faced the exasperation of being undiagnosed or have met medical professionals not equipped to manage your care. Taken to the extreme, some patients experience gaslighting or neglect.

### Finding Providers

Valued physicians practice medicine in a way that communicates trust and solidarity. This shared understanding makes the whole process easier and leads to better quality of care because both parties are respectful and listen to each other. It's critical to find the right doctor and medical team.

Find a physician who is knowledgable about your condition and wants to work with you. Studies show that communication style directly impacts patient trust, satisfaction, and perceived quality of care. Patients managing chronic illness benefit from long-term relationships with providers who communicate consistently and compassionately over time.

To find a doctor, get recommendations from physicians you trust, other patients, and your patient advocacy organization. Then, do some investigating to understand more about the physician's background and research they've done. Finding the right medical team can serve you for many years, so it's worth the time investment up front.

Some vetting must be done in person. Let the doctor know you want to build a true partnership and note the response. When seeing a doctor for the first time, ask how the office handles an after-hours question or medical need. During appointments, is there adequate time if you have several questions you want to ask the doctor?

Once you're working with a particular doctor, you'll be able to better assess the practice. Each physician has their own style of patient care that may or may not match what you prefer. It's OK to break up with a doctor and find another when you must. If you feel consistently unheard or dismissed, consider changing providers. Trust your intuition.

Sometimes you need a specialist and don't have a big menu of options. You may encounter a physician who lacks a good bedside manner or whose practice is poorly run, but you still need to see that particular specialist. Do your best to build an alliance with the doctor and staff so your health care remains the top priority.

Never put up with substandard treatment, but be mindful that doctors are human, too, and are dealing with their own stressors. Medical providers have bad days, like everyone else. Say something if an uncomfortable interaction is significant enough to potentially impact the relationship. Try to bridge the gap by attempting to clarify their recommendation, providing more detail about your symptoms, and asking for an alternative option.

Sometimes you must switch physicians simply because your case becomes more complicated. Though it can feel like starting from square one, learn how to shift and transition into new relationships with medical providers. It serves you well to be adaptable, so you get the right care from the right provider. How do you gracefully leave one practice for another? You can provide whatever statement you think is best. Let the doctor know you have appreciated their care. Leaving on good terms makes it less uncomfortable, especially if you see them or need their expertise again.

In addition to doctors, other key players include nurse practitioners, scheduling staff, and pharmacists. All play important roles. It's a great gift to know you are in partnership with professionals who are experts in their fields, take you seriously, always call you back, and are there when you need them. These essential relationships can be just as impactful as those with medical doctors. Be sure to thank these providers for their time. If someone goes out of their way to schedule you earlier for an appointment or provide some extra case management, let them know how much you appreciate their care.

### Medical Relationships and Rare Diseases

The diagnostic journey can take years, involving numerous referrals, misdiagnoses, and repeated invalidation. A 2022 global survey by EURORDIS found that the average time to diagnosis for rare diseases is more than five years, with nearly half of all patients receiving at least one incorrect diagnosis along the way.

This long road to answers could erode a patient's confidence in the medical system, especially if a provider ever doubted their physical symptoms or questioned their belief that something was wrong (gaslighting). Medical gaslighting occurs when a provider dismisses, downplays, or attributes legitimate physical symptoms to psychological causes. This is especially common with rare diseases, because doctors may not recognize a rare condition when they see it.

Patients and caregivers have been accused of exaggerating symptoms or, in extreme cases, of malingering or factitious disorder (formerly known as Munchausen syndrome). Such accusations prevent patients from accessing lifesaving care or seeking second opinions. These traumatic events can create profound mistrust and long-lasting emotional scars.

In certain contexts, patients and caregivers become "the expert" about a rare disease and must inform medical providers about the condition—in the emergency room, for instance. Always respect a provider's medical knowledge, while acknowledging that they may be unsure of how to treat you. Try to form an alliance by gently commenting on how rare your disease is, briefly describing how you are impacted, and suggesting they reach out to your specialist.

### Elena's Story

At thirty-two years old, Elena had been living with an undiagnosed autoimmune disorder for more than a decade. She cycled through doctors who minimized her symptoms or referred her elsewhere when answers were not easy. After years of searching, Elena finally met a rheumatologist who listened attentively, acknowledged her pain, and began piecing together the complex puzzle of her health. She finally received a diagnosis.

For the first time, she felt seen and validated. Yet, just as she was building trust, her doctor relocated out of state. Elena was back at the starting line—navigating a new specialist, more paperwork hurdles, and an old sense of uncertainty. Fortunately, she persevered and relied on a sense of serenity she had learned to cultivate from within.

While it was upsetting that her physician was moving, she finally had a clear diagnosis and had learned to advocate for herself. Elena could move forward, honoring her intuition and building trust one relationship at a time.

She knew how to ask the right questions, prepare in advance, obtain referrals from the autoimmune patient organization, and set up several appointments to find the right physician for her. Elena evenly spaced her appointments, so she was not overwhelmed by having to repeat her story. She even practiced in advance by role-playing with her caregiver, so she was ready to ask her list of questions.

### Medical Case Management

It's a tedious job, but you can advocate for yourself if you keep track of your medical records and serve as an accurate historian of your medical history. Documentation strengthens your position in discussions with medical providers. You can call upon these records in conversations with physicians and other providers, to ensure they make fully informed decisions about your care. Today, this means navigating a variety of patient portals and these platforms rarely talk to one another. In addition, you can create your own documentation. Consider creating these two important documents:

1. **A living medical history document**: Create and maintain a document that includes your diagnoses, medications, allergies, previous procedures, and provider contacts. This consolidated summary can reduce the stress of repeating your story at each appointment, which can also stir up uncomfortable memories and emotions. Your go-to document also prevents crucial details from being overlooked in transitions of care.

2. **A tracking list of symptoms and talking points**: You can foster a sense of agency with a document that records symptoms, documented communications, and questions you want to ask at the next appointment.

For people who have complex medical histories, the role of medical case management falls on the patient in ways like never before. Patients are often expected to share documents and manage coordination among providers. Long gone are the days when a primary care provider could manage many of a patient's health care conditions. Patients must sometimes act as intermediaries, which is challenging when many of us have, on average, five to eight different providers. It's a tall order to ensure everyone has what they need and stays on the same page.

### Maintaining Control in Medical Interactions

You likely have firsthand experience with unpredictable medical systems, delays, shifting treatment plans, and inconsistent provider responses. Uncertainty takes an emotional toll. Being left in limbo while waiting for test results, approvals, or care decisions can lead to heightened anxiety and emotional fatigue. Acknowledge this emotional challenge and then find ways to manage it.

Here's a powerful tool you can put in your toolbox: the ability to focus on what you can control. Amid uncertainty and imperfect systems, you can control how you communicate, how you prepare for appointments, and how you advocate for your needs. We don't control how others respond, but we can resolve to prepare well, be clear in what we say, and adopt a businesslike tone. It's an investment in preventing emotional exhaustion later.

No one likes to feel caught off guard, so strategize ahead of your next appointment so you can steer the interaction. Take these steps to prepare for appointments that could be difficult:

- Write down key questions and health goals in advance.
- Practice mindfulness or grounding techniques.
- Bring a trusted support person or advocate.
- Set boundaries when conversations become overwhelming or dismissive.

It can help to cast ahead to what the doctor might ask you. Having a few scripted lines at the ready can be helpful. For instance, the doctor you see today might question a decision made by another physician. You don't have to explain or defend it. You can ask the provider to coordinate with other relevant providers. Simply say, "I recommend you touch base with my referring physician, who can provide greater context."

Follow these additional best practices to communicate assertively—not to be confused with aggressively.

These guidelines help you express needs, ask clarifying questions, and follow up when concerns are not addressed:

- Use "I" statements ("I feel concerned when..." or "I need clarification on...").
- Reiterate what you heard ("Just to confirm, are you saying...?").
- Request notes or summaries to review later.
- Follow up with other pertinent questions you may not have been able to ask through the patient portal or via email.
- Schedule decompression time after appointments, as needed.

### Engage in Shared Decision-Making

Health care is full of hard-to-understand medical terms. But "shared decision-making" plainly says what it is. First, the patient must understand the basics about the condition and a potential treatment. Then, with a physician's counsel, the patient can gain an understanding of the risks and potential benefits.

Your doctor might already practice this style of communication, or you might want to learn about it yourself and recommend it. The approach allows the patient's voice to come through while leaning on the physician as the expert who provides evidence-based research needed for educated choices. Not surprisingly, patients who engage in shared decision-making processes report greater satisfaction and adherence to treatment.

"The optimal decision takes into account evidence-based information about available options, the provider's knowledge and experience, and the patient's values and preferences," according to the Agency for Healthcare Research and Quality (AHRQ).

The arrival of messaging and email between doctor and patient provides another way to communicate and increase collaboration. Do your part to foster a good relationship by writing short, clear messages. Providers are more likely to be responsive if they know email communication is used respectfully.

### Remember to Breathe and Other Calming Tips

Even with the best preparation and meticulous record-keeping, getting medical care can still be upsetting and cause trauma responses, especially for patients who have experienced health anxiety, medical trauma, medical gaslighting, or painful procedures. Mindfulness-based approaches and emotional regulation strategies reduce anxiety and improve communication in clinical encounters. Try these self-regulation strategies to support clear thinking and emotional safety:

- Box breathing or 4-7-8 breathing techniques (see Chapter 10)
- Holding grounding objects or stress-relief items
- Visualizing a calming image or saying a positive affirmation
- A quick bathroom break to reset if the visit becomes overwhelming

## Communication: The Heart of Healing

Clear, empathetic communication is one of the most powerful tools in the patient-provider relationship. Patients who feel heard are more likely to adhere to treatment plans, share critical health information, and return for follow-up care.

Medical relationships are not just transactional. They are emotional, layered, and deeply impactful for those living with chronic illness. Strengthening communication skills, advocating with intention, and grounding in internal control help you navigate even the most complex medical systems with more clarity and less emotional cost.

You deserve to be seen, heard, and respected—not only as a body to be treated but also as a person with insight and experience. When that happens in a healthy partnership with a medical team, healing takes on another dimension within a connected relationship.

NINE

# introduction to mental health

LIVING WITH A CHRONIC ILLNESS CHANGES everything. It reshapes how we experience our bodies, identities, and relationships. In addition to managing symptoms and navigating a complex medical system, we must also cope with psychological and emotional challenges that are often overlooked. Mental health and chronic illness are inextricably linked, and for those of us navigating these realities daily, the psychological impact is profound and deserves attention.

As we dive into the subject of mental health, I hope you'll keep the following in mind:

- Your symptoms—both emotional and physical—are real.

- Emotional care, education, and self-advocacy are acts of resilience.
- There is no perfect way to manage mental health—only the path that's right for you.

This is not about perfection. It's about connection, courage, and knowing that your story matters. Chronic illness often introduces factors beyond our control—disease progression, health, and medical policy changes. The goal is to be able to do the following:

- Recognize and manage stress and trauma responses
- Manage your nervous system when your body is on alert
- Utilize coping strategies, which lead to resilience

Meanwhile, many of us face these common mental health challenges in relation to chronic illness:

- Health anxiety and medical trauma
- Medical care burnout
- Gaslighting
- Delayed diagnosis or misdiagnosis
- Financial and insurance-related stressors

- Clinical mental health conditions, such as anxiety, depression, PTSD, and obsessive-compulsive disorder (OCD)
- Relationship issues and ruptures
- Caregiver burnout and changes in support systems
- Medical crises, flare-ups, and medical instability
- Isolation—physical and emotional
- Shifts in medical care team, or shame or misunderstanding from medical professionals
- Grief or loss
- Lack of understanding from others about rare diseases
- Managing the emotional regulation of loved ones

Living with a chronic health condition means living with uncertainty, which can cause a stress response. Can you distinguish between what you can and cannot control? That's critical for emotional resilience. Recognizing and focusing energy on internal control—our reactions, self-care, and communication—foster empowerment. You can decrease emotional exhaustion if you let go of "what ifs," fear-based thoughts, and long-term narratives that may not be serving you. Learning how to communicate your needs to others can also help you secure the support you actually need from your loved ones.

Drawing from my experience working with patients, caregivers, siblings, friends, and loved ones—as well as my own personal experience as a patient—this chapter reflects clinical understanding and lived truth.

If you're wondering what practical steps you can take, I'll address that in the next chapter. Also coming up, I'll talk about seeking professional help when you need it. In my opinion, mental health care is not a luxury—it is a lifeline.

As you reflect on your story, consider the following:

- What emotional impacts has your illness had on your identity or sense of self?
- What resources have helped you cope emotionally
- Have you experienced medical gaslighting?
- Have you experienced health anxiety or medical trauma?
- What support is helpful or unhelpful?
- Which relationships have shifted since your diagnosis?
- How do you show yourself compassion during flare-ups or difficult times?
- Where is their room for improvement and how do you start this journey?

## Understanding the Psychological Impact

As a therapist and a patient, I've witnessed firsthand how deeply health challenges affect mental health. Individuals living with chronic conditions often experience anxiety, depression, PTSD, grief, and a profound sense of loss over their previous selves and future dreams. The unpredictability of chronic illness can cause sustained distress, fear of progression or relapse, and disconnection from identity and community.

Invisible losses accumulate: missing celebrations, canceling plans, and explaining limitations. People we turn to may let us down. Some health care providers won't listen to us or believe us, leading to a feeling of being "gaslit." These experiences can feel isolating and invalidating.

But you can still find your agency in challenging situations. After more than twenty-five surgeries and navigating care as an immunocompromised patient, I've learned how to advocate for myself and use coping strategies, which decreases stress and gives me the head space to stay on top of appointments and medical regimens. This leads to better outcomes. For example, before a recent surgical procedure, I confidently requested infection-control accommodations. Years ago, this request would have caused anxiety, because I would have feared resistance from the medical team. The way I now handle such situations stands as a testament to my growth and empowerment.

If you feel your needs are being minimized, track symptoms, prepare notes, and assertively communicate. Seek providers who listen and validate.

### Managing Uncertainty and Stress

Medical outcomes, treatment plans, financial stability, and even daily functionality can fluctuate without warning. This uncertainty triggers the body's stress response, activating the sympathetic nervous system's fight-or-flight mode. Stress is unavoidable if you live with a chronic health care condition.

Over time, chronic activation can lead to emotional exhaustion, anxiety, and feelings of hopelessness. It's crucial to recognize uncertainty as a normal part of the chronic illness experience. Building resilience does not mean eliminating uncertainty but developing tools to manage it.

### Understanding Stress Versus Distress

Stress is the body's response to any demand. In distress, on the other hand, people experience uncomfortable, overwhelming emotions. You need not fear stress. Without some stress, we might never get out of bed, make the coffee, and do the normal routine of daily life. Everyday life stress can motivate positive coping, like taking the steps necessary to prepare for a medical appointment.

Scientific research shows the brain, endocrine system, vagus nerve, and immune system all influence mood and inflammation. Approaches informed by polyvagal theory have shown promise in supporting nervous system regulation and emotional stability in the face of chronic stress. Developed by Dr. Stephen Porges, polyvagal theory emphasizes the role of the vagus nerve in modulating our physiological state.

When individuals with chronic illness learn how to activate their parasympathetic ("rest and digest") response through breathwork, grounding, or safe social engagement, they are better able to manage physical symptoms and emotional reactivity. Trauma-informed care that incorporates this model can foster a sense of internal safety, which is essential for healing.

After COVID-19, many patients reported mood dysregulation and brain fog—even those who were previously stable. Research confirms the biological basis: neuroinflammation and hormonal disruption affect the prefrontal cortex and adrenal system.

And yet emotional stress, on its own, does not cause chronic illness. Stress can and does impact your ability to manage an illness. Frequent distractions pile up and eat up the day, leaving less time and energy to do the laundry, finish a work project, or make dinner. The whole experience can lower our tolerance for daily stressors and drain us of the energy needed to meet up with friends, exercise, or spend time on a hobby—the very activities that can improve mood.

Prolonged, severe, unresolved distress requires attention. High levels of stress can lead to clinical mental health conditions such as anxiety, depression, and PTSD, not only from the physical burden of the disease, but also from medical trauma, diagnostic delays, and being dismissed by health care professionals.

No one has to go it alone. You can learn to recognize when you tip from stress into distress. Use that as a prompt to seek additional support, adjust coping strategies, or engage professional mental health support.

## Medical Trauma, Health Anxiety, and PTSD

When I work with clients in my practice, I often explain the difference between stress and trauma. Whereas stress is a normal response to challenging life experiences, trauma is a response to harmful, threatening experiences, such as witnessing violence, or experiencing a catastrophe or an abusive relationship.

In medical trauma, a person has a physiological or psychological response to pain, injury, serious illness, medical procedures, a life-threatening event, or frightening treatment or diagnostic experiences. For many with chronic illness, medical trauma happens repeatedly since the situation is ongoing. They regularly have health flare-ups and must undergo tests, invasive procedures, and hospitalizations.

Repeated distress without support can lead to medical PTSD. Symptoms may include hypervigilance, emotional numbing, flashbacks, or panic. Caregivers also can experience trauma when they witness a loved one who is suffering or facing a life-threatening illness. Researchers call that an "enduring somatic threat." Trauma persists because the body continually reminds patients of past danger.

Medical trauma differs from other forms of complex trauma because the stressor comes from within. The body is sending an alert that something is wrong and sets off a fight-or-flight response, which can lead to increased mental health symptoms. Cortisol, memory, and stress signals alert us that we need to seek help.

We can't—and shouldn't—turn this response off. It's a necessary adaptive mechanism. What we can do is learn how to use coping mechanisms to decrease symptoms and increase tolerability. Each of us needs our resourceful nervous system, but we don't want it to overwhelm.

You may feel betrayed by your own body. The identity shift from being an able-bodied individual to one who lives with chronic illness can feel like a loss. You might grieve for your former self. Chronic illness may alter your social world, affect friendships, change roles in romantic relationships, or lead to social withdrawal. Those living with invisible illnesses and lesser-known diseases often have encounters that are invalidating, or cause isolation or feelings of emotional fatigue.

For those living with complex medical conditions, the burden of ongoing treatment can compound the psychological toll. Managing time-consuming health care, navigating insurance, and coordinating multiple specialists can be emotionally exhausting. What starts as overwhelming may eventually become routine, like brushing your teeth or showering, but the emotional labor should not be dismissed.

As challenging as it is, not all roads lead to despair. There's even a phrase for it: post-traumatic growth. This kind of growth happens because psychological changes occur as a result of the struggle with highly challenging life circumstances, such as chronic illness.

Many people emerge from hardship with increased resilience, purpose, and advocacy skills. In fact, traumatic health events may empower patients to take greater ownership of their care, communicate more clearly, and live with intention.

Our strength is in how we adapt, connect, and care for ourselves. Living with chronic illness often requires tremendous strength—navigating a complicated medical system, tolerating physical discomfort, and finding ways to still lead fulfilling lives. We deserve acknowledgment for this resilience. A new model of mental health support must center around the lived experience of patients and validate the emotional complexity of being a medical outlier.

## Grief, Loss, and Identity

Anyone living with a chronic illness can point to a list of what I call "invisible losses" that may not always be acknowledged by society, friends, or even loved ones. There are no cards or funerals for the things we've lost—stamina, former roles, or a sense of certainty in our lives. But the grief is real, and it is often cyclical. Chronic illness grief doesn't necessarily have a beginning, middle, and end. It can come in waves and be retriggered by health flare-ups, medical dismissals, or unmet milestones.

Chronic illness impacts identity in deep and often disorienting ways. Who we are is frequently tied to what we do, how we relate to others, and how we move through the world. When those aspects change—perhaps we can no longer work full-time, parent in the same way, or participate in activities that once brought joy—it can create a crisis of self. This doesn't mean we lose our core identity, but we are forced to adapt and reconstruct how we define ourselves.

Some may experience shame or guilt over needing accommodations or appearing different. Others may feel unseen, especially when symptoms are invisible or misunderstood. The loss of a coherent personal narrative—"This is who I am, this is what I do"—can lead to grief that is difficult to articulate even to those closest to us.

Ambiguous loss occurs when someone or something is physically present but psychologically changed—or vice versa. In chronic illness, this applies to the person experiencing the illness as well as their family. We may look the same but feel utterly different inside. We may mourn the loss of who we were before diagnosis or of relationships that couldn't withstand the changes.

Friends may drift away, careers may stall, and long-held dreams may be deferred. You may feel grief, not only for what has been lost but also for what will never be. This anticipatory grief is common when living with progressive or unpredictable illness. Each diagnostic test, time-consuming appointment, or missed social event due to symptoms can reignite a sense of mourning.

To move forward, we must give ourselves permission to name these losses. Writing about them, talking to a therapist, joining a support group, or creating rituals of remembrance can be powerful. These are not indulgences—they are necessities. The grief of chronic illness deserves just as much compassion and validation as any other form of loss.

Take the healing step of finding language to apply to your experience. Naming what we've lost puts us on track to reclaim what still remains.

## How Mood Affects Relationships and Functioning

When mental health declines—due to grief, trauma, depression, or burnout—it can affect every aspect of our lives. We may become withdrawn, misinterpret interactions, or react defensively. For individuals managing chronic illness, maintaining emotional regulation is critical to sustaining support systems and advocating effectively. Mental well-being is essential for relational stability.

When we are grounded, we are more capable of:

- Asking for help
- Setting clear boundaries
- Accepting support
- Articulating needs and limitations clearly

In the next chapter, we talk about how to stay grounded and explore a variety of practical strategies that can help you strengthen your coping muscles. It takes practice and delivers results. When you improve your ability to cope and bounce back, you win back some of your time. That's time you can fill with the people and activities you find enjoyable and meaningful.

TEN

# strategies for managing mental health

You've arrived at what could be the most impactful chapter in the book—an organized guide for practical coping strategy options. I recommend a variety of strategies you can use right now. You'll also see different options for professional mental health support, if you decide to take that path. I provide a list of evidence-based modalities. It's OK if some suggestions resonate and others don't. Pick and choose what works best for you.

Let's start with easy-to-do activities. The following activities can improve brain health and lower stress by producing mood-enhancing endorphins and decreasing cortisol associated with fight-or-flight nervous system responses:

- Exercise and physical movement
- Creative expression, such as a hobby
- Physical touch
- Joyful distractions
- Music
- Community support to include connection with friends and family
- Routines and structure
- Time spent in nature

Some of the evidence-based coping strategies I suggest may be familiar to you. Even if you have tried these approaches before, take this opportunity for a fresh start. Research backs up their effectiveness. I have seen them work for my clients, for fellow patients, and in my own experience.

### Stay Grounded—Exercises for Emotional Regulation

When you're overwhelmed, grounding exercises can give your brain something new to focus on, interrupting the emotional swirl. These essential strategies reconnect you to the present moment. Try these two simple but effective techniques:

- **5-4-3-2-1 Exercise:** Name five things you can see, four things you can feel, three things you can hear, two things you can smell, and one thing you can taste.

- **Box Breathing:** Inhale for four counts, hold for four counts, exhale for four counts, and hold for four counts. Repeat until a sense of calm returns.

Grounding daily, even when feeling well, builds a reserve of emotional regulation that can be called upon during moments of distress.

### Start (or Restart) a Mindfulness Practice

For many of us, a mindfulness practice can feel a bit out of reach. Maybe you've tried it and couldn't make it a regular habit. Or did you give it a go but were never sure if you were doing it right? Anyway, how can you add this extra task to your already-full plate? Know that it's worth your time to try again.

Mindfulness practices, such as bringing attention back to the breath, sensations, or surroundings, can be vital in managing uncertainty and emotional overwhelm. Mindfulness can anchor us in the present moment, reducing catastrophic thinking and emotional spirals often triggered by unpredictable chronic illness flare-ups.

It can be as easy as using an app or finding one of the many mindfulness exercises on YouTube. Start with a short exercise and build this muscle over time. For example, focus on feeling gratitude for being well enough to attend an event. You don't have to adopt a formal mindfulness practice.

### Take a Healthy Approach to Social Media

Social media can be a double-edged sword for individuals managing chronic illness. It offers community and information but can also fuel comparison, misinformation, and emotional burnout. Use it as a tool of empowerment by taking these precautions:

- Curating your feed to include uplifting and supportive content
- Taking intentional breaks from news and health forums as needed
- Setting time limits to avoid doomscrolling
- Being mindful about how online information impacts your emotional state

**Improve Insight**

It can feel intimidating to begin taking stock of your stresses and emotional health. But you can start the process with something as simple as a regular check-in with yourself. Ask yourself the following four questions. Consider journaling about the answers. Do you spot any patterns?

- Am I irritable due to a specific issue, or is everything bothering me?
- Have I lost interest in meaningful activities?
- Are my thoughts stuck in hopeless loops?
- Are my symptoms medical, emotional, or both?
- Am I staying connected to family and friends, or am I isolating?

## Take Up Journaling

Something shifts ever so slightly when you write down your thoughts and feelings. The act of journaling could be helpful to you, and there are no rules. You don't have to show anyone what you wrote or keep the pages. Experiment by letting the mind go with a journaling exercise. Sometimes the process of expressing our feelings can feel cathartic. Embrace what has changed and the resilience that comes from adapting. You might feel a bit lighter afterward.

1. What do I feel gratitude for?
2. What are my goals?
3. If I could look at something from a different perspective, what would it be?
4. How has my chronic health condition impacted me?
5. What is something I wish people knew?

## Try Mood-Tracking Tools and Apps

Mood-tracking can help patients observe connections between emotions, physical symptoms, and daily events. Useful tools include these:

- **Daylio** (mood logging and patterns)
- **Mood Mission** (suggests evidence-based coping skills)
- **Moodkit** (CBT-focused journaling)
- **Insight Timer** and **Headspace** (guided mindfulness)

### Experience the Power of Reframing and Self-Compassion

We all "frame" our experiences, often without thinking about it. Learning to reframe lets us see the situation through a more empowering lens. You might say or think to yourself, *I failed because I needed help*. But you could look at it differently with a reframed thought: *I showed strength by recognizing when I needed support*.

Through reframing, we can practice self-compassion and meet our struggles with kindness rather than criticism. Treating ourselves with gentleness fosters recovery, connection, and hope. It's the path to emotional resilience, which is much in demand when you're living with a chronic illness. These are not traits that we're born with. They are skills you can develop. You can work on them on your own or seek help from a professional.

### Three Steps to Cope with Negative Thinking

In those moments when you feel overwhelmed by the weight of negative feelings, try these steps:

1. **Acknowledge and validate your feelings.** Denying difficult emotions only leads to shame. Admitting that you're struggling—especially during medical or health-related stress—can offer a sense of relief and connection.

2. **Interrupt negative spirals.** When triggered by stress, our brains default to familiar negative thought cycles. Identifying that "thoughts are just thoughts" and not absolute truths can help. Use a written or digital list of reframing strategies to strengthen this skill.

3. **Take action.** Rather than fixating on *why* you feel bad, instead ask, *What can I do right now to shift my state?* Positive distraction, such as an activity, social interaction, or mindful breathing, can interrupt the stress response and reengage the task-focused brain.

## Resilience-Building Tips

- Remember your talents and abilities and remind others of them.
- Establish a self-care routine that supports your health.
- Strive for competency in managing your health—it takes organization and savvy to navigate the medical system.
- Learn how to adapt to change.
- Accept the course of your condition without giving up hope of some relief.
- Seek peer and community support.
- Utilize mental health resources.

## Should You See a Therapist?

How validating it is to live in a time when we have more access to mental health resources. Options include mood trackers, mindfulness apps, and peer support communities. Journaling, talk therapy, grounding exercises, creative outlets, and supportive communities also play essential roles.

These tools do not cure, but they make life more livable, more connected, and less lonely. Friends, too, are essential sources of support. Even so, there may come a time when you struggle with symptoms your friends aren't equipped to handle. You may need help from a mental health provider.

If that's you, know that you have these professional mental health resources:

- **Individual therapy** for processing trauma, grief, clinical mental health symptoms, and managing relationships
- **Support groups** for validation and solidarity, can be peer or therapist led and does not require an ongoing commitment
- **Couples therapy** for caregiving and relationship dynamics
- **Group therapy**, a therapist led process in a closed group environment
- **Family therapy** to address interpersonal dynamics with parents, siblings, and patients
- **Psychiatric assessment** for psychotropic medication evaluation
- **Genetic testing** for psychotropic medications

A skilled therapist can help guide you through the complicated ways biology, psychology, and social dynamics intersect in your unique experience of illness.

Therapeutic approaches should be tailored and sensitive to your needs at different stages of your journey—not one-size-fits-all. Whether it's medical trauma, post-traumatic stress, grief, anxiety, depression, or adjustment to a new diagnosis, chronic illness often demands a tailored approach. Most important is that you find a therapist you feel comfortable with and who feels like a good fit.

Mental health therapy relies on a variety of evidence-based approaches to address the stressors related to chronic health care conditions. Please note that the suggested modalities below may change with additional research after this book is published. This section is meant to be a guide:

### Evidence-Based Mental Health Therapies for Chronic Illness

- ACT (Acceptance and Commitment Therapy): helps patients accept ongoing health challenges and align actions with personal values.

- Cognitive Behavioral Therapy (CBT): provides tools to identify and challenge unhelpful thinking patterns.

- **Cognitive Processing Therapy (CPT)**: trauma-focused therapy adapted for medical trauma and post-traumatic stress following chronic illness or intensive care.

- **Compassion-Focused Therapy (CFT)**: reduces shame and self-criticism, supporting resilience in patients with chronic illness and pain.

- **Dialectical Behavior Therapy (DBT)**: offers skills for emotion regulation, mindfulness, and distress tolerance.

- **Emotionally Focused Therapy (EFT)**: an attachment-based couple therapy with strong evidence for improving relational resilience in couples coping with chronic illness.

- **Family and Couple Interventions**: structured programs that improve communication, coping, and support among patients, partners, and caregivers.

- **Interpersonal Psychotherapy (IPT)**: evidence-based for depression, grief, and role transitions in chronic medical conditions.

- **MBCT (Mindfulness-Based Cognitive Therapy)** and **MBSR (Mindfulness-Based Stress Reduction)**: structured mindfulness programs that promote present-moment awareness, reduce anxiety, and prevent depressive relapse.

- **Meaning-Centered Psychotherapy (MCP)**: rooted in logotherapy, helps patients find purpose and growth despite illness; well-researched in oncology and palliative care.

- **Narrative Therapy**: reframes illness stories, supporting meaning-making and reclaiming agency.

- **Somatic modalities** (e.g., **Somatic Experiencing**, **Sensorimotor Psychotherapy**): body–mind approaches for processing stress and trauma; not appropriate for all medical conditions.

- **Trauma-Informed Care**: a guiding framework that prioritizes safety, regulation, and empowerment in the context of stressors and medical trauma.

Modalities like CBT, ACT, MBSR, DBT, and TIC offer evidenced-based pathways to healing. Choose what resonates with your needs. Note that some somatic methods may not be suitable for all chronic illnesses.

As we continue to advocate for ourselves within the health care system, we must acknowledge that mental health care is not a luxury but a necessity. The psychological impact of chronic illness is real, valid, and deserving of clinical attention and compassion. Through therapy, peer support, and emotional tools, we can reclaim our narratives and build lives rooted in resilience, self-compassion, and hope.

Validation is powerful. When patients feel heard, believed, and supported by their mental health providers, they are more likely to engage in treatment and experience relief. Each person's psychological response to chronic illness is shaped by their unique history, personality, social support, and experiences with the health care system. Therefore, mental health care must be personalized and holistic.

Healing is not linear. Flare-ups happen. Setbacks occur. Even with every skill in place, chronic illness is still exhausting. But you don't have to do it alone.

## *How to Shape Your Brain*

Thanks to neuroplasticity, a natural function, your brain changes and adapts based on experience and repeated thought patterns—just like physical exercise reshapes muscles. Chronic stress, shame, and trauma activate two core brain networks:

- The **default mode network (DMN)** is associated with negative thinking, self-criticism, isolation, and depressive symptoms.

- The **task mode network (TMN)** is engaged when we focus on external activities, goals, and present-moment awareness, reducing negative thought loops.

Social influences, including trauma and stress, shape how our brains operate. Repeated exposure to emotional pain or neglect can heighten DMN activity, whereas targeted interventions, such as mindfulness or therapeutic exercises, help retrain neural pathways, boosting emotional resilience and self-efficacy.

Chronic illness often activates the DMN through stress and pain, which activates the amygdala, where our fight-or-flight responses originate. But therapeutic tools, such as mindfulness, CBT, and grounding, can help shift brain activity toward the TMN. This switch supports better problem-solving, emotional regulation, and resilience by strengthening pathways to the frontal lobe, where flexibility, empathy, and insight are housed.

# acknowledgments

This book represents the culmination of my life's work in the chronic illness and rare disease space. I wrote it with deep passion and care. I set out to educate patients so they can access the evidence-based mental health support they're seeking. I also wanted to create a resource for mental health and medical professionals, so they are well equipped to assist chronically ill patients seeking their care.

I close with a note of gratitude. Most important, to the reader, this may be the end of this book, but it is not the end of the conversation. I will continue sharing, learning, and advocating alongside the patient community. I hope you found this book to be relatable and validating. Perhaps you will return to a section when the days feel long and uncertain. Maybe you will share it with a loved one and it will bridge a gap between the two of you. In relationships, I remain a fierce optimist, always hopeful, always believing there is room for growth.

Here's one last exercise to try: Take a moment today to identify one relationship that sustains you. Nurture it. Reach out. We heal best in connection.

As a therapist, I am a holder of stories. It's been a privilege to hold the stories of so many patients and caregivers in individual, group, couples, and family therapy. I'm forever grateful to the chronic illness community and the friendships I've formed there. I don't see this as "trauma bonding." Human beings connect through shared experiences, and living with chronic health conditions is a unique kind of experience. Having others who simply get it—who lead without judgment and offer real understanding—has been vital to me.

I'm also deeply thankful for all the people who allow me to live a full life. I could not have done this without them. In these pages, I focus on managing and strengthening relationships to build resilience and community. I need that. We all need that.

I thank my caregivers—throughout all stages of my life—who have stood by me during surgeries, diagnoses, and day-to-day health flares. This includes my parents, my significant other Sean, and the very special friends who stepped in when I wasn't well. I especially thank

Sean, my partner and caregiver during the last nine years. It has not been easy, but without your care and love, all of this would not be possible.

And to my medical team—Dr. Wellington Tichenor, Dr. Thomas J. Walsh, and nurse practitioner Mary Youch—thank you for being just a phone call away. You have worked tirelessly, beyond nine-to-five boundaries, to help me maintain quality of life and freedom. I'm grateful, too, to the physician specialists who embraced the complexity of my rare disease with curiosity, dedication, and willingness to collaborate. That is the true meaning of medicine and patient care.

To my editor, Debra Moffitt, your guidance made this project possible—and without your inspiration, my book notes may have remained dormant for another decade. I also thank biotech company CSL, not only for developing lifesaving biologics, but also for recognizing the importance of mental health and well-being in improving the lives of people living with rare, serious, and chronic diseases.

# about csl

*CSL is proud to help bring Jodi Taub's voice and vision to more patients living with chronic illnesses. By supporting the creation and distribution of this book, CSL champions the health and emotional resilience of the patients we serve.*

CSL (ASX:CSL; USOTC:CSLLY) is a leading global biopharma company with a dynamic portfolio of lifesaving medicines, including those that treat hemophilia and immune deficiencies, vaccines to prevent influenza, and therapies in iron deficiency, dialysis and nephrology. Since our start in 1916, we have been driven by our promise to save lives using the latest technologies. Today, CSL provides lifesaving products to patients in more than 100 countries and employs 29,000+ people. Our unique combination of commercial strength, R&D focus and operational excellence enables us to identify, develop and deliver innovations so our patients can live life to the fullest.

For inspiring stories about the promise of biotechnology, visit *csl.com/vita.*

For more information about CSL, visit *csl.com*.

# notes

*Chapter 1*

Global Wellness Institute. 2023. *2023 Global Wellness Economy Monitor: Data for 2019–2022.*

Keller, Richard M., and C. E. Galgay. 2010. "Microaggressive Experiences of People with Disabilities." In *Microaggressions and Marginality: Manifestation, Dynamics, and Impact*, edited by Derald Wing Sue. Wiley.

Linehan, Marsha M. 2015. *DBT® Skills Training Manual*. 2nd ed. Guilford Press.

McEwen, Bruce S. 2007. "Physiology and Neurobiology of Stress and Adaptation: Central Role of the Brain." *Physiological Reviews* 87 (3): 873–904.

Nakao, Mutsuhiro, Kentaro Shirotsuki, and Nagisa Sugaya. 2021. "Cognitive–Behavioral Therapy for Management of Mental Health and Stress-Related Disorders: Recent Advances in Techniques and Technologies." *BioPsychoSocial Medicine* 15 (1): 16.

Rosenberg, Marshall B. (2015). *Nonviolent Communication: A Language of Life*. 3rd ed. PuddleDancer Press.

Woodberry, Kristen A., Kaitlin P. Gallo, and Matthew K. Nock. 2008. "An Experimental Pilot Study of Response to Invalidation in Young Women with Features of Borderline Personality Disorder." *Psychiatry Research* 157 (1–3): 169–80.

## *Chapter 2*

Alsarrani, Abdullah, Ruth F. Hunter, Laura Dunne, and Leandro Garcia. 2022. "Association between Friendship Quality and Subjective Wellbeing: A Systematic Review." *BMC Public Health* 22: 2420.

Beetz, Andrea, Kerstin Uvnäs-Moberg, Henri Julius, and Kurt Kotrschal. 2012. "Psychosocial and Psychophysiological Effects of Human-Animal Interactions: The Possible Role of Oxytocin." *Frontiers in Psychology* 3: 234.

Camero, Katie. "How to Make New Friends as an Adult When You Have a Chronic Illness." *SELF*, May 20, 2024.

Capela e Silva, Fernando, Emily Kieson, Alexandra N. Stergiou, and Inês Pereira Figueiredo. 2024. "Editorial: How Animals Affect Us: Examining the Influence of Human-Animal Interactions on Human's Health." *Frontiers in Veterinary Science* 11: 1509960.

Chopik, William J. 2017. "Associations Among Relational Values, Support, Health, and Well-Being across the Adult Lifespan." *Personal Relationships* 24 (2): 408–22.

Gmeiner, Michael W., and Adelina Gschwandtner. 2025. "The Value of Pets: The Quantifiable Impact of Pets on Life Satisfaction." *Social Indicators Research* 178: 185–223.

Janevic, Mary R., Varick Shute, Cathleen M. Connell, John D. Piette, Jenna Goesling, and Julie Fynke. 2019. "The Role of Pets in Supporting Cognitive-Behavioral Chronic Pain Self-Management: Perspectives of Older Adults." *Journal of Applied Gerontology* 38 (9): 1276–1300.

McNicholas, June, and Glyn M. Collis. 2006. "Animals as Social Supports: Insights for Understanding Animal-Assisted Therapy." *British Journal of Social Work* 36 (5): 623–41.

Odendaal, Johannes S. J., and Roy Albert Meintjes. 2003. "Neurophysiological Correlates of Affiliative Behaviour between Humans and Dogs." *The Veterinary Journal* 165 (3): 296–301.

Pezirkianidis, Christos, Evangelia Galanaki, Georgia Raftopoulou, Despina Moraitou, and Anastassios Stalikas. 2023. "Adult Friendship and Well-Being: A Systematic Review of PERMA Perspectives." *Frontiers in Psychology* 14: 990270.

Purewal, Rebecca, Robert Christley, Katarzyna Kordas, et al. 2017. "Companion Animals and Child/Adolescent Development: A Systematic Review of the Evidence." *International Journal of Environmental Research and Public Health* 14 (3): 234.

Taub, Jodi. "9 Ways to Support Your Friend with a Rare Disease." Jodi Taub Therapy Blog, 2022.

### *Chapter 3*

Baxter, Leslie A., and Dawn O. Braithwaite. 2008. "Metadiscursive Practices in Couples' Talk about Illness: Enacting 'Health as Normal' and 'Health as Crisis' Narratives." *Qualitative Health Research* 18 (1): 5–17.

Pachankis, John E. 2007. "The Psychological Implications of Concealing a Stigma: A Cognitive-Affective-Behavioral Model." *Psychological Bulletin* 133 (2): 328–45.

Quinn, Diane M., and Stephanie R. Chaudoir. 2009. "Living with a Concealable Stigmatized Identity: The Impact of Anticipated Stigma, Centrality, Salience, and Cultural Stigma on Psychological Distress and Health." *Journal of Personality and Social Psychology* 97 (4): 634–51.

### *Chapter 4*

Ainsworth, Mary D. Salter, Mary C. Blehar, Everett Waters, and Sally N. Wall. 1978. *Patterns of attachment: A psychological study of the strange situation*. Lawrence Erlbaum.

Bowlby, John. 1982. Attachment (Attachment and Loss Series, Vol. 1). 2nd ed. Basic Books.

Farrell, Allison K., A. Lea Stimpel, Sarah C. E. Stanton, and Richard B. Slatcher. 2023. "Relationship Quality and Physical Health: Responsiveness as an Active Ingredient Predicting Health across the Lifespan." *Current Opinion in Psychology* 52: 101507.

Gottman, Julie Schwartz, and John M. Gottman. 2015. *10 Principles for Doing Effective Couples Therapy*. W. W. Norton & Company.

Gottman, John M., and Nan Silver. 2015. *The Seven Principles for Making Marriage Work: A Practical Guide from the Country's Foremost Relationship Expert*. Harmony.

Levine, Amir, and Rachel S. F. Heller. 2010. Attached: The New Science of Adult Attachment and How It Can Help You Find—and Keep—Love. TarcherPerigee.

Martire, Lynn M., and Vicki S. Helgeson. 2017. "Close Relationships and the Management of Chronic Illness: Associations and Interventions." *American Psychologist* 72 (6): 601–12.

Merz, Erin L., Vanessa L. Malcarne, Celine M. Ko, Melody Sadler, Lisa Kwack, James W. Varni, and Georgia Robins Sadler. 2011. "Dyadic Concordance among Prostate Cancer Patients and their Partners and Health-Related Quality of Life: Does It Matter?" *Psychology & Health* 26 (6): 651–66.

Mikulincer, Mario, and Phillip R. Shaver. 2016. *Attachment in Adulthood: Structure, Dynamics, and Change*. 2nd ed. The Guilford Press.

Pietromonaco, Paula R., and Nancy L. Collins. 2017. "Interpersonal Mechanisms Linking Close Relationships to Health." *American Psychologist* 72 (6): 531–42.

Rolland, John S. 1994. "In Sickness and in Health: The Impact of Illness on Couples' Relationships." *Journal of Marital and Family Therapy* 20 (4): 327–47.

## *Chapter 5*

Bonacaro, Antonio, Chiara Cosentino, Concetta Collaro, et al. 2025. "Experiences of 'Indirect' Illness in Family Caregivers of Chronically Ill and Older Adults: A Qualitative Study." *International Journal of Environmental Research and Public Health* 22 (2): 240.

Litzelman, Kristen, Erin E. Kent, Michelle Mollica, and Julia H. Rowland. 2016. "How Does Caregiver Well-Being Relate to Perceived Quality of Care in Patients with Cancer? Exploring Associations and Pathways." *Journal of Clinical Oncology* 34 (29): 3554–61.

Monin, Joan K., and Richard Schulz. 2009. "Interpersonal Effects of Suffering in Older Adult Caregiving Relationships." *Psychology and Aging* 24 (3): 681–95.

Tatkin, Stan. 2023. *In Each Other's Care: A Guide to the Most Common Relationship Conflicts and How to Work through Them*. Sounds True.

*Chapter 6*

Bryson, Brooke A., and Kathleen R. Bogart. 2020. "Social Support, Stress, and Life Satisfaction among Adults with Rare Diseases." *Health Psychology* 39 (10): 912–20.

Davenport, Liam. 2022. "Genetic Testing for Best Antidepressant: Accurate, Cost Effective. *MDedge*.

Edmondson, Donald. 2014. "An Enduring Somatic Threat Model of Posttraumatic Stress Disorder due to Acute Life-Threatening Medical Events." *Social and Personality Psychology Compass* 8 (3): 118-34.

Forkey, Heather, Moira Szilagyi, Erin T. Kelly, and James Duffee. 2021. "Trauma-Informed Care." *Pediatrics* 148 (2): e2021052580.

Kazak, Anne E., Nancy Kassam-Adams, Stephanie Schneider, Nataliya Zelikovsky, Melissa A. Alderfer, and Mary Rourke. 2006. "An Integrative Model of Pediatric Medical Traumatic Stress." *Journal of Pediatric Psychology*, 31(4): 343–55.

Lerch, Matthew F., and Susan E. Thrane. 2019. "Adolescents with Chronic Illness and the Transition to Self-Management." *Journal of Adolescence* 72 (1): 152–61.

Schulz, Richard, and Paula R. Sherwood. 2008. "Physical and Mental Health Effects of Family Caregiving." *American Journal of Nursing* 108 (9 Suppl): 23–27.

Smith, Ben J., and Michelle H. Lim. 2020. "How the COVID-19 Pandemic Is Focusing Attention on Loneliness and

Social Isolation." *Public Health Research and Practice* 30 (2): 3022008.

Taub, Jodi. "How Long Should Parents Be Caregivers?" CSL, June 29, 2023.

Taub, Jodi. "Patient Advocacy Tools: Mental Health and Caregiver Fatigue" [Video presentation]. Project ECHO, Penn State College of Medicine, December 15, 2023.

Uhlenbusch, Natalie, Bernd Löwe, Martin Härter, Christoph Schramm, Christina Weiler-Normann, and Miriam K. Depping. 2019. "Depression and Anxiety in Patients with Different Rare Chronic Diseases: A Cross-Sectional Study." *PLOS ONE* 14 (2): e0211343.

Vitaliano, Peter P., Jianping Zhang, and James M. Scanlan. 2003. "Is Caregiving Hazardous to One's Physical Health? A Meta-Analysis." *Psychological Bulletin* 129 (6): 946–72.

Wendlandt, Blair, Liam Pongracz, Feng-Chang Lin, et al. 2023. "Posttraumatic Stress Symptom Trajectories in Family Caregivers of Patients with Acute Cardiorespiratory Failure." *JAMA Network Open* 6 (4): e237448.

## *Chapter 7*

Choi, Jin. Young., Seon Heui Lee, and Soyoung Yu. 2024. "Exploring Factors Influencing Caregiver Burden: A Systematic Review of Family Caregivers of Older Adults with Chronic Illness in Local Communities." *Healthcare* 12 (10): 1002.

Pashazade, Hakime, Masoomeh Maarefvand, Yadollah Abolfathi Momtaz, and Kianoush Abdi. 2024. "Coping Strategies of the Sandwich Generation in the Care Process: A Qualitative Study." *BMC Public Health* 24: 20327.

Pinquart, Martin, and Silvia Sörensen. 2006. "Gender Differences in Caregiver Stressors, Social Resources, and Health: An Updated Meta-Analysis." *The Journals of Gerontology: Series B* 61 (1): P33–P45.

Schulz, Richard, and Paula R. Sherwood. 2008. "Physical and Mental Health Effects of Family Caregiving. *American Journal of Nursing* 108 (9): 23–27.

Xiong, Chen, Melissa Biscardi, Arlene Astell, et al. 2020. "Sex and Gender Differences in Caregiving Burden Experienced by Family Caregivers of Persons with Dementia: A Systematic Review." *PLOS ONE* 15 (4): e0231848.

## *Chapter 8*

Beach, Mary Catherine, Debra Roter, P. Todd Korthuis, et al. 2013. "A Multicenter Study of Physician Mindfulness and Health Care Quality." *Annals of Family Medicine* 11 (5): 421–28.

Černe, Tina, Lijana Zaletel Kragelj, Eva Turk, and Danica Rotar Pavlič. 2024. "Experiences of Quality of Life and Access to Health Services among Rare Disease Caregivers: A Scoping Review." *Orphanet Journal of Rare Diseases* 19: 319.

Dhedhi, Saadia Aziz, Deborah Swinglehurst, and Jill Russell. 2014. "'Timely' Diagnosis of Dementia: What Does It Mean? A Narrative Analysis of GPs' Accounts." *BMJ Open* 4 (3): e004439.

Elwyn, Glyn, Dominick Frosch, Richard Thomson, et al. 2012. "Shared Decision Making: A Model for Clinical Practice." *Journal of General Internal Medicine* 27 (10): 1361–67.

Epstein, Ronald M., and Richard L. Street. 2007. *Patient-Centered Communication in Cancer Care: Promoting Healing and Reducing Suffering*. National Cancer Institute, NIH Publication No. 07-6225.

Ha, Jennifer Fong, and Nancy Longnecker. 2010. "Doctor-Patient Communication: A Review." *Ochsner Journal* 10 (1): 38–43.

Safran, Dana Gelb, William Miller, and Howard Beckman. 2006. "Organizational Dimensions of Relationship-Centered Care: Theory, Evidence, and Practice." *Journal of General Internal Medicine* 21 (S1): S9–S15.

Schmoyer-Edmiston, Nic, and T. Richards. 2025. "Recognizing and Addressing Medical Trauma: An Imperative for Integrated Primary Care." *Families, Systems, & Health.* [Advance online publication.]

Shire. 2013. *Rare Disease Impact Report: Insights from Patients and the Medical Community.*

Stepanian, Natalie, Marie Hamilton Larsen, Joshua B. Mendelsohn, Kari L. Mariussen, and Kristin Heggdal. 2023. "Empowerment Interventions Designed for Persons Living with Chronic Disease: A Systematic Review and Meta-Analysis of the Components and Efficacy of Format on Patient-Reported Outcomes." *BMC Health Services Research* 23: 911.

Street, Richard L. Jr., Howard Gordon, and Paul Haidet. 2021. "Physicians' Communication and Perceptions of Patients: Is It How They Look, How They Talk, or Is It Just the Doctor?" *Social Science and Medicine* 273: 113767.

Zikmund-Fisher, Brian J., Angela Fagerlin, and Peter A. Ubel. 2022. "Risky Feelings: Why a 6% Risk of Cancer Doesn't Always Feel Like 6%." *Patient Education and Counseling* 81(Suppl): S87–S93.

*Chapter 9*

Åsbring, Pia, and Anna Liisa Närvänen. 2002. "Women's Experiences of Stigma in Relation to Chronic Fatigue Syndrome and Fibromyalgia." *Qualitative Health Research* 12 (2): 148–60.

Campbell, Mari, Alex Clarke, Andrew Symes, Sarita Workman, Hans Stauss, and A. David Webster. 2018. "Investigating the Effectiveness, Acceptability and Impact on Healthcare Usage of Providing a Cognitive-Behavioural Based Psychological Therapy Service for Patients with Primary Antibody Deficiency." *Clinical Immunology* 191: 68–76.

Gambadauro, Pietro, Vladimir Carli, and Gergö Hadlaczky. 2019. "Depressive Symptoms among Women with Endometriosis: A Systematic Review and Meta-Analysis." *American Journal of Obstetrics and Gynecology* 220 (3): 230–241.e1.

Manusama, Olivia R., Nico J. M. van Beveren, P. Martin van Hagen, Hemmo A. Drexhage, and Virgil A. S. H. Dalm. 2022. "Psychological Symptoms in Primary Immunodeficiencies: A Common Comorbidity?" *Journal of Clinical Immunology* 42 (3): 695–98.

McEwen, Bruce S., and Eliot Stellar. 1993. "Stress and the Individual: Mechanisms Leading to Disease." *Archives of Internal Medicine* 153 (18): 2093–101.

Miller, Andrew H., and Charles L. Raison. 2016. "The Role of Inflammation in Depression: From Evolutionary Imperative to Modern Treatment Target." *Nature Reviews Immunology* 16 (1): 22–34.

Porges, Stephen W. 2022. "Polyvagal Theory: A Science of Safety." *Frontiers in Integrative Neuroscience* 16: 871227.

Scott, Kate M., Carmen Lim, Ali Al-Hamzawi, et al. 2021. "Association of Mental Disorders with Subsequent Chronic Physical Conditions: World Mental Health Surveys from 17 Countries." *JAMA Psychiatry* 78 (2): 150–58.

Sebring, Jennifer C. H., Christine Kelly, Deborah McPhail, and Roberta L. Woodgate. 2023. "Medical Invalidation in the Clinical Encounter: A Qualitative Study of the Health Care Experiences of Young Women and Nonbinary People Living with Chronic Illnesses. *CMAJ Open* 11 (5): E915–E921.

Tedeschi, Richard G., and Lawrence G. Calhoun. 2004. "Posttraumatic Growth: Conceptual Foundations and Empirical Evidence." *Psychological Inquiry* 15 (1): 1–18.

### *Chapter 10*

Davidson, Richard J., and Bruce S. McEwen. 2012. "Social Influences on Neuroplasticity: Stress and Interventions to Promote Well-Being." *Nature Neuroscience* 15: 689–95. 10.

Gheshlagh, Reza Ghanei, Kourosh Sayehmiri, Abbas Ebadi, Asghar Dalvandi, Sahar Dalvand, and Kian Nourozi Tabrizi. 2016. "Resilience of Patients with Chronic Physical Disease: A Systemic Review and Meta-Analysis." *Iranian Red Crescent Medical Journal* 18 (7): e38562.

Kralik, Debbie, Antonia van Loon, and Kate Visentin. 2006. "Resilience in the Chronic Illness Experience." *Educational Action Research* 14 (2): 187–201.

# about the author

Jodi Taub, LCSW, PLLC, is a New York–based psychotherapist with over 27 years of experience providing individual, couples, family, and group therapy. She specializes in chronic illness and rare diseases, supporting patients and caregivers in managing health anxiety, medical trauma, and the psychological impact of complex health conditions.

In addition to her clinical work, Jodi is a published writer, speaker, and researcher. She lectures nationally, facilitates support groups, and contributes to professional education and advocacy within the chronic illness and rare disease communities. Drawing on both her expertise and her own lived experience with chronic illness, Jodi is recognized for her evidence-based, relationship-centered approach that fosters resilience and meaningful connections.

www.ingramcontent.com/pod-product-compliance
Lightning Source LLC
Chambersburg PA
CBHW031325230926
51848CB00001B/97
* 9 7 8 1 9 6 7 1 1 5 2 5 9 *